Endorsements

T. W. S. Hunt can write, and he understands his topic. His book will give real help to believers working their way through the winter he describes.

~J. I. PACKER
Theologian and best-selling author of *Knowing God*

T. W. S. Hunt is the best of both worlds—a true writer and a true thinker. He is poetic in his expression, profound in his thought, and biblical in his passion. *Winter with God* displays moments of brilliance and creativity that mark the marvelous debut of a young, up-and-coming writer who deserves to be noticed and read.

~GARY THOMAS
Best-selling author of *Authentic Faith* and *Sacred Marriage*

T. W. S. Hunt has the three qualities I most value in a spiritual writer: honesty, depth, and verve. *Winter with God* crackles with surprising images, a lively play of language, and probing commitment to truth. An auspicious debut from a vibrant new voice!

~MIKE MASON
Author of *The Gospel According to Job*

The combination of rich, poetic writing and practical, forthright questioning makes this book unique. It will warm the hearts of those in winter.

~S. C. WILLIAMS
Author of *The Shaming of the Strong*

WINTER

WITH

GOD

BroadStreet Publishing Group, LLC
Racine, Wisconsin, USA
BroadStreetPublishing.com

WINTER WITH GOD: *Hope for the Spirit, Strength for the Soul*

Copyright © 2016 T. W. S. Hunt

ISBN-13: 978-1-4245-5298-6 (hardcover)
ISBN-13: 978-1-4245-5299-3 (e-book)

Unless otherwise indicated, all Scripture references are taken from The ESV® Bible (The Holy Bible, English Standard Version®), copyright © 2001 by Crossway, a publishing ministry of Good News Publishers. All rights reserved. Scripture marked NLT is taken from the Holy Bible, New Living Translation, copyright © 1996, 2004, 2015 by Tyndale House Foundation. Used by permission of Tyndale House Publishers Inc., Carol Stream, Illinois 60188. All rights reserved. Scripture marked NIV is taken from THE HOLY BIBLE, NEW INTERNATIONAL VERSION®, NIV® Copyright © 1973, 1978, 1984, 2011 by Biblica, Inc.® Used by permission. All rights reserved worldwide. Scripture quotations marked NRSV are taken from the New Revised Standard Version Bible, copyright © 1989 the Division of Christian Education of the National Council of the Churches of Christ in the United States of America. Used by permission. All rights reserved. Scripture marked KJV is taken from the King James Version of the Bible.

Stock or custom editions of BroadStreet Publishing titles may be purchased in bulk for educational, business, ministry, fundraising, or sales promotional use. For information, please e-mail info@broadstreetpublishing.com.

Cover design by Chris Garborg, garborgdesign.com
Typesetting by Katherine Lloyd at www.theDESKonline.com

Printed in China
16 17 18 19 20 5 4 3 2 1

WINTER

WITH

GOD

40-DAY DEVOTIONAL

Hope for the Spirit,
Strength for the Soul

T.W.S. HUNT

BroadStreet
PUBLISHING

For my mother.
You gave me literacy,
I give you literature.

Contents

One must have a mind of winter …
[To see] nothing that is not there
and the nothing that is.

Wallace Stevens, *The Snow Man*

Spiritual Winter

> You always expect to be sad … each year when the
> leaves fell from the trees and their branches were bare
> against the wind and the cold, wintry light. But you
> knew there would always be the spring, as you knew
> the river would flow again after it was frozen.
>
> *Ernest Hemingway, A Moveable Feast*[1]

Shakespeare's *Richard III* doesn't say that now is the winter of our *contentment*. Quite the opposite, winter is the season of our "discontent."[2] Winter is the graveyard of the entire year: all of spring, summer, and autumn are buried deep within it. And long after Christmas carols have ceased to be sung, many of us are still singing, "I really can't stay (But, baby, it's cold outside)."[3]

Winter is something we learn to live with and live through. We have to because it lasts a quarter of the calendar year or much longer if, like me, you live in Canada! Still, the season has its charms. As Ralph Waldo Emerson said, "For the attentive eye, each moment of the year has its beauty."[4] In Canada, sunny winter skies unveil themselves in champagne brightness, the air is crisp and fine like cut crystal, and ice turns waterways into highways. Also, the skiing is superb! But more than any other season, winter is one we watch from behind a window. It's the season we long for least, and the one we're least sad to see go.

So too, with our spiritual winters—our days of discontent: when God's divine light rises late and sets early. In such times, nothing seems to grow. Where warmth once abounded, things come to feel frigid. And the landscape of our lives—whether it's felt within or without—appears colorless, formless, and lifeless.

Whereas we can predict a meteorological winter's beginning and end, there's no methodology for when we winter with God. For us, seasons *with* God feel like what time is *to* God. As Peter wrote, "A day is like a thousand years, and a thousand years are like a day" (2 Peter 3:8 NIV). There's simply no telling when winter with God will end. We only know that it will end in this life or the next.

The spiritual work of winter is to survive the cold by keeping warm one's love for God. We mustn't try to avoid this spiritual season—praying, as in Scripture, "that it may not happen in winter" (Mark 13:18). Because it's in winter that we learn to love God out of season, or rather, in spite of the season. It's then that we stop asking *from* God and instead ask *for* God. And in the bleak midwinter, we begin to fathom what it means to love God with all of one's being.

This slim volume of spiritual meditations is wintry in its outlook. It points to the ways in which grace descends upon life, like a soft, quiet snowfall. It wants to walk beside you in the cold and show you the fresh footsteps of Jesus. And it aims to fan dying embers into living flames, to stoke the fires of refinement in order to ignite a life of discipleship. For in this chilly and darkened season, God has given us the gift of fire. Jesus is the spark, and we are the kindling. To keep warm, we must burn with love, and to see far, we must burn very brightly.

This book recommends that we throw everything into the flames—starting with ourselves—so that everything will be illuminated and transformed by the Refiner's fire. But rest assured, we shall neither be scorched nor singed. As the prophet Isaiah promised, "When you walk through the fire you shall not be burned, and the flame shall not consume you" (Isaiah 43:2). The light of the fire is only meant to see us through the winter and the warmth of its blaze to keep us till the spring.

Winter with God is best explored chronologically over the span of days and weeks. This slow and considered approach—reading one chapter at a time—will gradually expose you to the forces of spiritual reformation. Like weathering on a rock, it will reshape you in new and unexpected ways. Into what exactly, or whom, neither the author nor the reader can know. I only hope this book will help you through your spiritual winter. I pray that you will evermore live in God, and God will even more live in you.

1

Faith Alone?

> If I have all faith, so as to remove mountains,
> but have not love, I am nothing.
>
> *1 Corinthians 13:2*

On November 7, 1940, the 2,800-foot-long carbon steel torso of the Tacoma Narrows Bridge unraveled amidst moderate to strong winds. A YouTube video shows the gigantic bridge eerily waltzing with the wind, writhing and weaving, and then violently it disintegrates and descends into the waters of Puget Sound. In the video, however, the trees in the foreground and background seem unbothered by the wind: the bridge breaks but the trees barely bend. This is a result of the wind's external frequency matching the bridge's natural structural frequency. The bridge collapsed—not by accident—but by (poor) design, because the resonant frequencies of the wind and the bridge coincided, thus creating a natural mode of vibration. In essence, the wind did to the bridge what a soprano's voice could do to a glass; it shattered.

Similarly, faith in Jesus Christ is the frequency that shakes the world. His Spirit "blows where it wishes" (John 3:8), and when it does, things tremble. It can turn a Saul into a Paul, water into wine, empires into ashes, and death into life. As Jesus said, "If you have faith like a grain of mustard seed, you will say to this mountain, 'Move from here to there,' and it will move, and nothing will be impossible for you" (Matthew 17:20).

Faith is a mystery. But when the mystery moves, mountains do too: physical disease, debilitating doubt, cultural atrophy, national apostasy, entrenched evil, even death itself. They are all cast into the sea. And yet, whose prayers can move mountains? Mine certainly don't. But it does seem like tremors can be felt when we genuinely pray, "Not my will, but thine, be done" (Luke 22:42 KJV).

Our faith is atomic: powerful in its potential but minuscule in its size. It's the one atom we seem unable to split. But how might we? How can faith believe all it's been told? How can it assume "the assurance of things hoped for, the conviction of things not seen" (Hebrews 11:1)?

To begin with, the solution is not found through believing harder or becoming more mystical. Nor is faith best augmented through signs and wonders, because faith can't actually believe in everything. As Paul wrote, it's "love … [that] believes all things" (1 Corinthians 13:7). Love also bears all things, hopes all things, and endures all things. Faith doesn't exist apart from love but through it. So if we want more faith, we should pray for more love: the love of God, love for God, and love for one another.

Application: When we feel loved, we feel like loving. Reflect on who or what has made you feel truly loved.

Supplication: Jesus, my Friend, give me both faithful love and loving faithfulness. Help my faith to reach up to you by reaching out to my neighbor. Give me your eyes to see the invisible; your hands to help the hapless; your heart to love the loveless; and through loving them, may we both love you. Come, Holy Spirit. Amen.

2

How Long?

The LORD has made everything
for its purpose.

Proverbs 16:4

The human desire for purpose is as natural as our need for food. If we have a purpose, we can get by with little else; as Nietzsche wrote, "He who has a why to live can bear almost any how."[1] But the opposite is also true. He who has no purpose has no how or why to live. After all, "Hope deferred makes the heart sick" (Proverbs 13:12). When King David couldn't discern any purpose behind his suffering, he cried out, "How long, O Lord? Will you forget me forever?" (Psalm 13:1). And how long will it be for us until the life we believe that we were made for becomes the one we actually get to live? How long will it be until we see God's purposes come to fruition in what we do, whom we love, where we live, and who we are?

The answer to "how long?" might be very long. The biblical

imagery for life and growth is organic, seasonal, and perennial. The growth of a vine, for instance, is gradual. A new vine takes three years before its branches can produce the first grapes fit for wine, and it takes another seven years of pruning before reaching full production. "Be patient, therefore," wrote James. "See how the farmer waits for the precious fruit of the earth … until it receives the early and the late rains" (James 5:7). Be patient, when there is no rain at all—no hope of purpose or fulfillment in life—because in times of drought a vine's roots grow stronger as it digs for moisture. In the future, the wine produced by these grapes tastes better, not worse, for having experienced drought. And the same is true for the dryness we experience when our lives seem to lack direction or meaning. The absence of purpose can produce an abundance of character because who we are isn't dependent on what we do.

Jesus said, "If you remain in me and I in you, you will bear much fruit" (John 15:5 NIV). This harvest might come when the conditions seem just right, when the vines are ready to be picked, and the wine to be produced. Instead, the harvest might be delayed until winter—when our hopes and dreams are frozen on the vine—because God has a special vintage in mind. This will probably seem like too little or too late, but as every spiritual sommelier knows, God is, in fact, making ice wine: an exquisite drink of terrific sweetness, which is produced through terrible stress.[2] As Adam Gopnik explains, "Every winter, the grapes … are left [on the vine] not merely to chill but to freeze … and the brutal cold forces all the natural sugar into the core of the grape, where it waits to be pressed out."[3] So long as the fruit remains on the vine, the temporary pain contributes to the winemaker's true purpose: the world's most remarkable wine.

Application: It's hard to persevere when you feel as if you lack a purpose. So indulge yourself with a wholesome pleasure by cooking your favorite meal and invite God to dine with you.

Supplication: Lord, I need you. I need you more than my words can convey, more than my thoughts can comprehend, and even more than my desires can command. Most of all, I need to recall that I already have you—whether or not I feel you now—because you gave yourself to me long ago. Thank you that I am not actually alone; thank you that you are with me always: forever now, and forever more. Come, Holy Spirit. Amen.

3

Blessed

Whoever does not bear his own cross
and come after me cannot be my disciple.
For which of you, desiring to build a tower,
does not first sit down and count the cost …?

Luke 14:27–28

In the medieval period, it was assumed by some scholastic theologians that the virgin birth was a painless ordeal because Jesus Christ was a perfect baby. They reasoned that the effects of original sin were absent since Jesus was without sin. Today, this idea seems a little ludicrous. Why, for instance, would the incarnation, the act of God becoming human, sidestep the very pain that is part and parcel of being human? But as odd as it seems, we sometimes operate under very similar assumptions because we often expect God's gifts to be delivered to us without delay or labor. And when we ask to be blessed, we don't usually expect there to be any unwanted or painful side effects.

In one sense, we needn't be too concerned about such things because the Bible says that God gives good gifts to those who ask for them. God does indeed give us good gifts (like marriage … and beer and whiskey!). But God's gifts are not always our gifts, just as His ways are not necessarily our ways. Since God chooses to work good out of evil, it shouldn't surprise us if we get mixed blessings. After all, Jesus did say, "Blessed are the poor in spirit, for theirs is the kingdom of heaven" (Matthew 5:3).

We should be wary of blessings that seem to get us what we want without actually bringing us closer to God. Just as Dietrich Bonhoeffer argued in *The Cost of Discipleship* that there is "cheap grace," so too are there "cheap blessings." But while it's completely true that God often and gladly bestows on us the things that we desire—great and small, material and immaterial—He doesn't always do so. This is sometimes because the thing that we most need, which is a close relationship with God, actually grows best amidst the things we like the least. For just as absence makes the heart grow fonder, so hardship helps the heart grow stronger.

We're often told to count our blessings but rarely to count their cost. Perhaps we should, because many blessings don't come cheap. In fact, they only come connected to a life of discipleship, which requires us to pick up and carry our cross; and while that's life at its absolute best, it isn't life at its easiest either. We might do ourselves a favor then if we looked long and hard at what kind of blessing we really want. Is it God's blessing or just our own?

Application: List the three innermost desires of your heart and reflect on them.

Supplication: Heavenly Father, more than health and happiness, beyond wealth and wisdom, above sanctity and security, help all of me to want all of you. Come, Holy Spirit. Amen.

4

A More Abundant Life

Jesus, when he began his ministry,
was about thirty.

Luke 3:23

A life lived as Jesus lived can be truly unremarkable. The vast majority of it might be incredibly normal, seemingly uneventful, and at times quite boring. After all, nine-tenths of Jesus' life was spent in small-town Nazareth, engaged in ostensibly ordinary things like learning, working, sleeping, eating, and spending time with family and friends.

If you want to imitate Jesus, you must be ready, like the meek, to inherit a world filled with normalcy. Being "on fire" for Jesus isn't all miracles and ministry or transfigurations and trials. In fact, it is quite the opposite. As C. S. Lewis put it, to "imitate God ... our model is the Jesus, not only of Calvary, but of the workshop, the roads, the crowds, the clamorous demands and surly oppositions, the lack of all peace and privacy, [and] the interruptions."[1] Following Jesus includes undesirable things like early mornings, lost earnings, and caring about the inane problems of others. But its lack of excitement is what separates faith from fantasy like wheat from chaff. Which is one reason why Paul was willing to moonlight as a tentmaker when he was officially in Corinth as a missionary. Indeed, most of the time, "God doesn't call us to do extraordinary things, but to do ordinary things with extraordinary love."[2] And God, in turn, endows each moment of ordinary life with His own eternal and extraordinary love.

Real devotion is grounded in real life. As Isaiah said, "Seek the Lord [where] he can be found" (Isaiah 55:6). Such devotion doesn't restrict itself to Scripture and religious ceremony but eagerly seeks God's glory in amongst life's little drudgeries, like doing the dishes. Its express aim is to "do all to the glory of God" (1 Corinthians 10:31). As such, true devotion is as content being in the valleys living for God's glory as it is being on the mountaintops living in God's glory. Whatever pleases the Lord is well with such a soul.

If we're unwilling to seek God in the life we have, we'll do no better in the life we'd like to have. False sanctity feverishly seeks ways to honor God in the future. Genuine faithfulness preoccupies itself with the present. It focuses more on what it will do, not what it could do. This is also much less interesting and exciting, but it is also more important. For real devotion is sometimes hardest to find, not when it is dangerous or demanding, but when it is ordinary and boring.

Application: Talk to someone you admire about how they made it through life's many doldrums and still remained faithful to God.

Supplication: Lord, if faith is boring, help me to bore through it. If hope is for the present, help me to hope presently. If love is for real life, help me to really love. And if this is the only way that life can be truly lived, help me to live it, Jesus, because you are the way, the truth, and the life. Come, Holy Spirit. Amen.

5

How Do We Pray?

One of his disciples said to him,
"Lord, teach us to pray, as John taught his disciples."

Luke 11:1

Prayer is a gratuitous, fortuitous, and tremendous gift. But in order for it to be enjoyed, it needs to be opened gratefully, intimately, forthrightly, and transformatively.

Prayer is a spiritual present intended for everyone, but it is unwrapped by few. This is why so-called prayer warriors are so hard to find. But why should this be? "Prayer is a gift," wrote Thomas Merton, and perhaps, "it is given to so few because so few desire it, and of those who received it, so few have received it with gratitude."[1] In order to unlock the power of prayer, therefore, a heartfelt thank-you is just as important as a frequent amen.

Shakespeare wrote, "What's in a name?"[2] Not a lot, he thought, but there is in God's name. God lets us call Him, "Abba Father," which isn't a title but a truth. God is our Dad.

"Our Dad, who art in heaven" is more fatherly than any father, more loving than any love, and He knows us better than we know ourselves. We are His children, and He encourages us to talk to Him that way—needily, confidently, and intimately.

God wants us to pray through our emotions not around them. We can shoot, or rather pray, from the hip. The prayers of the Psalms, for instance, can be unhesitatingly and unnervingly honest:

You have put me in the depths of the pit. (88:6)
Your wrath lies heavily on me. (88:7)
How long will you hide your face from me? (13:1)
I suffer your terrors; I am helpless. (44:24).

This is because the psalmist understands that real prayer, however raw, won't rattle God. Mark Twain once wrote, "Under certain circumstances, urgent circumstances, desperate circumstances, profanity provides a relief denied even to prayer."[3] But Mark Twain was wrong: true prayer can be as forthright as profanity and just as colorful.

True prayer is also transformational. But it changes us, not God, because God is already more loving than we can fathom, more just than we can comprehend, and more merciful than we dare imagine. Indeed, why would we want to change God? The message of prayer is that it's the sender, not the receiver, who needs to change. But real prayer isn't about us altering ourselves. Instead, it is the Holy Spirit who creates in us the likeness and loveliness of God. True prayer seeks the radical and unconditional willingness to simply be transformed by God.

Application: Pray for the courage to speak honestly to God about something you've previously downplayed, denied, or kept from Him. For inspiration, watch either the full program or just the ending of *The West Wing* episode "Two Cathedrals."

Supplication: Jesus, please help me to pray with brutal honesty. If I need to scream and shout, give me volume. If I need to cry and weep, give me tears. Please supply whatever I require, so long as it's my desire, to adore you with my whole heart, soul, strength, and mind. Come, Holy Spirit. Amen.

6

A Prayer
of Bereavement

Precious in the sight of the Lord
is the death of his saints.

Psalm 116:15

Heavenly Father,
the passing of your saints,
which is precious to you,
is painful for us.

You may console our loss,
but you don't return the lost.
They are joyed to be with you—
we are grieved to be without them.

Our prayer isn't for the dead,
so much as for the living.

Help us not to hate the world,
its design, or its designer.

You did not say, "Live well,
and life will end well."
But, "Love me,
and life will last forever."

Heal our anger,
and help us to adore.
We often forget, Lord,
you went through this before.

Amen.

Application: In a handwritten letter, explain to God and explore for yourself what you felt and thought when you were most grieved.

Supplication: Lord, I know life takes but let my spirit give. Memories fade but let my gratitude grow. Lives end but let my love outlast. I go but let my life live on. Come, Holy Spirit. Amen.

7

If God Is Dead

The LORD is near the brokenhearted
and saves the crushed in spirit.

Psalm 34:18

The Lisbon Earthquake of 1755 was one of the deadliest tremors in history. The earthquake produced a tsunami in the Atlantic Ocean, an inferno in the city, and robbed the world of 100,000 people. The long list of casualties also included the early-Enlightenment's idea of God: a reasonable and benevolent creator who had constructed the best of all possible worlds. For how could such a God be true, it was reasoned, if such calamities befell innocent and unsuspecting people?

When we experience storms, earthquakes, and fires—literally or figuratively—we often react like the philosophers of Europe. The certainty of evil makes us question the reality of God, or at least a God who claims to be good. And in the wreckage of whatever we're experiencing, whether it's sickness, loneliness, bereavement, or failure, we often find the remains of the God we hoped for, the God who only allows good things to happen to those who love Him.

So what should we do when God seems dead, absent, or altered? The Bible suggests that in addition to maintaining faith, hope, and love, we can complain. A lot. In fact, we have the power of prayer for such times as these—not to suppress our concerns but to express them! This is what the psalmist (or alarmist) does in over half the Psalms. He cries out to God: telling God to act more like God. But there is a difference between a true and false complaint—between lamenting and grumbling—and this difference is trust. We must always believe in the ultimate goodness of God because it is the very basis of our appeal.

A heartfelt complaint begins with a heart full of gratitude. Those who rejoice in the presence of something show a deeper appreciation for it than those who merely complain in its absence. And those who celebrate life—the splendor of every second and exquisiteness of every inch—possess a greater seriousness when they grieve the loss of it. So if a momentary disaster besets us, we should cry out to God and make our complaint known, but we should also call out in praise for every moment of truth, goodness, happiness, and beauty. The latter will surely outweigh the former. For even at the heart of grief is gratitude, and at the core of a complaint is celebration.

Application: In a given day, there might be a hundred things that make you feel grateful but only a few things for which you express gratitude. Give thanks today for everything to everyone, everywhere, and every time it is due.

Supplication: God, in good times, give me gratitude. In bad times, grant me fortitude. Just whatever you do, please get me through—through to you. Come, Holy Spirit. Amen.

8

The Cold Church

I am with you, to the end of the age.

Matthew 28:19

Winter is a season of solidarity. People come together—less by attraction than compulsion—because the season's longevity and frigidity force them to find comfort in the company of one another. In winter, we learn, as individuals, that we're not self-sufficient. We need each other. But winter, as a spiritual season, is more isolating. In the coldness of God's apparent absence, we tend to batten down the hatches, to hibernate apart from the group, or trudge off alone into the unknown darkness. We need others, but we choose isolation.

In winter, the church is meant to be a source of warmth and camaraderie because we can huddle together around the light of Christ. More often, however, the church feels like an igloo: a shelter made from ice and snow, which is supposed to protect us from ice and snow. It might offer temporary refuge, but many don't want to stay too long. After all, being in a faith setting can be difficult if our faith is faltering. Nobody wants to "fake it till they make it." Nor do they want to stick around in a culture where ineptitude, monotony, and hypocrisy seem to be so common.

Yet, for all the good reasons to leave the church, there are even better reasons to stay. Apart from the fact that the church is seldom amended by abandoning it, nor the abandoner improved apart from it, the fact that the church is deeply flawed is relatively good news. It demonstrates just how unfailing God's crazy love is for such a sorry group of people.

God always keeps His family close, and we're to do likewise. As Augustine reportedly said, "The Church may be a whore, but she is my mother." Certainly, the church has occasionally put her faith in progress over providence, but she's still the mother of our hope. The church may have given to Caesar things that are God's, and vice versa, but she's still the matriarch of grace and salvation. Indeed, she's done many things wrong, even when there was every reason and resource to do right, but God's fidelity to her is forever. Surely, then, if our terrible mother has received such wonderful love from our Father—the kind that always lasts and never fails—there's every reason to hope for their struggling children. In fact, spending our winter within the church makes us a part of the greatest guarantee imaginable; for Jesus promised, "I will not leave you as orphans; I will come to you" (John 14:18). Indeed, God will come by the winter's end, and in the meantime, we can prepare our hearts for His arrival.

Application: Pick something you do not like about church and pray to God about it. In a week or two, revisit the issue.

Supplication: Forgive me, Jesus, if my individual relationship with you devolves into an isolated relationship. You gave your life in order to gather us together into one family, not so that I could live my life apart from others. Please return us, your runaway children, just as you recovered the famous lost sheep. Come, Holy Spirit. Amen.

9

Twinkle, Twinkle, Little Star

When [the wise men] saw the star, they rejoiced
exceedingly with great joy.

Matthew 2:10

The stars are the script of God's nightly love letter to us;
and the one hundred million stars of the Milky Way
are the glint of God's eye. When the ancients beheld them
with their naked eyes, they asked, "What is man that you
are mindful of him?" (Psalm 8:4). Today, the question should
be reversed because who are we that we're not more mindful of God? We may browse the night sky with sophisticated
sight and science, but somehow we're becoming increasingly
desensitized to the wonder. If one star brought the wise men
bowing before Christ, why does a full night sky not bring
everyone's hearts and minds back to God?

Perhaps it's because we lack stillness—which is a cure that

we so often treat as a curse. As Blaise Pascal wrote, "The sole cause of man's unhappiness is that he does not know how to sit quietly."[1] Instead, we must gain momentum by standing still. "Be still," the Lord says, "and know that I am God" (Psalm 46:10). Be still because we need to sit quietly below the stars in order to be awed by them into wonder and the worship of God.

It may be, however, that we lack proper perspective. Because in order to see God above, we also need to search for Him within. It is no use, in Augustine's words, to go "abroad to wonder at the heights of mountains … [or] the circuits of the stars, yet pass over the mystery of [oneself] without a thought."[2] For woven within every man and woman is the mystery of God's own image. To see the kingdom of God without, we must first look within.

So we have eyes but don't always see; and sometimes we can see but aren't bothered to look. At such moments, we are willfully unaware of God's presence, because we're unwilling to invest more than a moment's notice in nature's splendor and sublimity. We fail to appreciate what we've been given because we haven't the foresight to imagine it being taken away. As Ralph Waldo Emerson once wrote, "If the stars should only appear one night in a thousand years, how men would believe and adore; and preserve for many generations the remembrance of the city of God which had been shown!"[3] But instead, the stars appear every night, and we barely glance at them. But if we looked again—with eyes of awe and wonder—we'd see that the love of God is writ large across the entirety and enormity of the night sky.

Application: Spend ten minutes stargazing. If you live in the city and can't see the stars, find a beautiful place to go for a walk and try to engage your different senses.

Supplication: Lord, thank you for filling the world with your grandeur and glory. Please help me to be more attentive, turning my amazement into admiration, my admiration into awe, and transforming my awe into adoration. Come, Holy Spirit. Amen.

10

Mea Culpa

Therefore, confess your sins to one another.

James 5:16

For those who've experienced the warming glow of a winter fire or heard the crackling whispers of burning logs, they know that there's no better way to keep hearth and home. Except, perhaps, for the inconvenience of finding, splitting, and storing firewood—as there's nothing worse than tending a dying fire on a cold, snowy night when the wood supply is stashed outside.

In the spiritual season of winter, when God seems as distant as summer, very few explanations satisfy our sense of lost or dormant relationship with Him. Perhaps this season is meant to test us somehow, teach us something, or humble us in some way. But it's also possible that the flame has been extinguished because we've sinned through selfishness or thoughtlessness, or accidentally, almost as if by virtue, or vice, of being human.

The act of true confession produces a catharsis as rich and warm as an evening fire, but the process or prospect of confession is about as unappealing as the midnight search for firewood. We all fear the dark and despise the cold because that's where we've hidden the things that we're ashamed of. But to rekindle our relationship with God, we will need to step foot into the snow and gather together our confessions like kindling for a fire.

Dietrich Bonhoeffer believed that when we recognize ourselves as sinners, we experience more liberation, not less. "[God] wants to see you as you are," wrote Bonhoeffer. "He wants to be gracious to you. You do not have to go on lying to yourself ... as if you were without sin; you can dare to be a sinner."[1] In fact, we can dare to be sinners before both God and each other. But given the choice, most of us would prefer to confess in silence to God, rather than out loud to another person. But why should it be easier to confess our imperfections to a perfect God, than reveal our flaws to another flawed human being? Is it not reasonable to expect their kindness, sympathy, and acceptance? Or could it be that when we confess privately that we occasionally allow ourselves to cut corners and not face certain facts? Is it possible when we confess inside ourselves that sometimes we are only confessing to ourselves? "Have we," wrote Bonhoeffer, "been confessing our sins to ourselves and granting ourselves absolution?"[2] Have we not become the people we ought to be—forgiven, healed, and happy—for fear of the people we have been? If so, then we have a confession to make—both to ourselves, to each other, and to God.

Application: To confront our demons, we must confide in angels. Talk to your pastor, priest, or perhaps a friend or family member about something you've kept hidden from yourself or God.

Supplication: Father, within me there is transgression; please forgive it. There are wounds; please heal them. There is silence; please speak to it. There is love; please receive it. Indeed, Lord, take all of me and give me all of you. Thank you for all of this and more. Come, Holy Spirit. Amen.

11

Pilate's Prayer

Pilate said to him, "What is truth?"
After he said this, he went back outside.

John 18:38

Part of prayer is the things we say to God. So one might say, Pilate prayed (be it in earnest or in jest) because he asked Jesus, "What is truth?" But Pilate only prayed in part, since he left Jesus—not without an answer—but before he could hear it. Such was Pilate's folly (among many others). But maybe we shouldn't judge him too harshly, lest we be judged too. Because we often pray like Pilate: we ask for guidance but then go it alone, or we pray for God's will and then will whatever we want. Like Pilate, we feel comfortable talking to Jesus but uncomfortable listening to Him.

Prayer is partly what we say to God, but the other part is what God says to us. In the words of Hans Urs von Balthasar, "Prayer is dialogue, not man's monologue before God."[1] So we should try to listen to Jesus as much as we want Jesus to listen to us: heeding His voice quietly in contemplation, studiously in Scripture, inquisitively through study, attentively in service, occasionally in fasting, and continually in prayer. It may be rare to have time for this, but this is because we don't make time for it. But when we listen to God with our lives, we can say with more than our lips, "Speak, Lord, for your servant is listening" (1 Samuel 3:10 NIV).

How we prepare for prayer is sometimes as important as what we pray. John Cassian, the grandfather of Western monasticism, considered it an "inexorable fact that the condition of the soul at the time of prayer depends upon what shaped it beforehand."[2] Preparation, however, is less about the ordering of our words than the reordering of our hearts—for "a broken and contrite heart, O God, you will not despise" (Psalm 51:17). But the ultimate focus isn't on what we can do; instead, it's on what God is doing. "For it is God who works in you, both to will and to work for his good pleasure" (Philippians 2:13).

Listening for God prepares us for obeying Him. This is essential because God's still small voice rarely commands our attention, but it always requires our response. "Today," says the Word of God, "if you hear his voice, do not harden your hearts" (Hebrews 3:15). But we shouldn't mistake our response for an easy formality. The history of Israel cautions us against the notion that miracles and signs—even the voice of God—can guarantee our faithfulness. As the Bible says, "Who were those who heard [God's voice] and yet rebelled? Was it not all those who left Egypt led by Moses?" (Hebrews 3:16).

Application: Prepare your heart and mind for prayer by listening to a calming, contemplative song. Possible tracks include Taizé's "Jesus, Remember Me," Aaron Copland's, "Appalachian Spring, Track 1: Very slowly," or Kronos Quartet's, "The Beatitudes."

Supplication: Lord, I am listening, but please help me to listen longer than the length of this prayer. Come, Holy Spirit. Amen.

12

Why Do We Pray?

Seek first the kingdom of God and his righteousness,
and all these things will be added to you.

Matthew 6:33

God made reality with prayer in mind. It's an essential part of the infrastructure of everyday life. In fact, prayer is as much (and more) a language of reality as mathematics, chemistry, or physics. The supernatural and the natural are not separate in Christ—for all reality is His reality. As such, God invites us to pray about everything, not as if it were so, but because it is so.

Prayer may seem otherworldly, but it is decidedly this-worldly. If it weren't, Paul wouldn't tell us to "pray without ceasing" (1 Thessalonians 5:17), to "pray in the Spirit at all times" (Ephesians 6:18 NLT), and to "devote ourselves to prayer" (Acts 6:4). For prayer is a reliable resource in so far as we rely on God.

A rich prayer life—or rather, a life of prayer—is not the pinnacle of devotion. It's the foundation. There isn't a saint who's known for not praying or a revival that began without it. So we can't expect further progress in our spiritual lives without substantive prayer. But we can't all be saints, right? Then again, we can't exactly set the bar lower. Christ, whom we're to imitate, rose early and often, in order to pray earnestly and in solitude.

Prayer is only so good at getting what we want. But if we trust God, we're assured we'll get what we need. As Jesus Himself promised, "Your Father knows what you need before you ask him" (Matthew 6:8). Prayer, on the other hand, is excellent at getting what God wants. As 1 John attests, "This is the confidence we have in approaching God: that if we ask anything according to his will, he hears us" (5:14 NIV). So progress in prayer isn't necessarily when we get what we ask for, but when we trust God enough to ask Him for whatever He wants.

Prayer doesn't exclude personal requests, but they aren't its essence. At the heart of prayer, or in the heart of whoever prays, is a crossroads. To the left, we try to change God, and get Him to do things; to the right, we seek to be changed by God, and to do things for Him. One is the way of discipleship, the other isn't. That's not to say we can't ask God for things! Jesus invites us to, and says, "If you ask me anything in my name, I will do it" (John 14:14). But we should examine our prayers and determine *for* whose name are we asking. Do our prayers flow from loving God before ourselves, or for ourselves?

Application: Write a short letter to God, inquiring about what brings Him happiness and satisfaction.

Supplication: Lord, I trust you for what I need; I ask you for what you want. Come, Holy Spirit. Amen.

13

Are We Forgiven?

Father, forgive them,
for they know not what they do.

Luke 23:34

Is it possible to be too quick to ask for God's forgiveness? We wouldn't think so. It's not as though it was ever too soon for the Prodigal Son—from the Father's caring perspective—to return home. And preachers and prophets rightly say, "Let the wicked forsake his way. ... Let him return to the LORD, that he may have compassion on him" (Isaiah 55:7). But hastiness isn't necessarily godliness—as the Lord said, people can "draw near with their mouth and honor me with their lips, while their hearts [remain] far from me" (Isaiah 29:13).

God is always quick to forgive, but we can be slow to repent. We often prefer forgiveness in haste and repentance at leisure. A famous example of this is Augustine's prayer:

"Grant me chastity and continence, but not yet."[1] And many of us will likewise pray today for tomorrow's repentance. It's not that our hearts our wayward. We desire a way home, but we want to return by the path of least resistance. We often seek forgiveness without repentance in much the same way some seek health without exercise or grades without studying. We desire the end result, but we're deterred by the effort required to achieve it.

Repentance often seems too strenuous to undertake. It can feel as though we have to sort out all the deficiencies in our heart, soul, strength, and mind before we can turn back to God. Thankfully this isn't so. We don't have to sort ourselves out any more than patients have to heal themselves before they see a doctor. Our moral and spiritual regeneration is the fruit of repentance, not its seed. As Jesus said, "It is not the healthy who need a doctor, but the sick. I have not come to call the righteous, but sinners" (Mark 2:17 NIV).

The act of repentance begins with God, not us, "for it is God who works in us, both to will and to work for his good pleasure" (Philippians 2:13). His grace is what frees us from the impossible task of trying to make ourselves lovable through self-improvement. This doesn't exempt us from repentance; instead, as Paul says, "God's kindness is meant to lead you to [it]" (Romans 2:4). God still requires our confession and eventual reformation—but not from afar—we can return, like the Prodigal Son, long before we've improved. While God doesn't want us to avoid repentance anymore than He wants us to avoid Him, He does want to welcome us home and to assist our efforts to be conformed to Christ. Even if they begin with little more than the helpless cry "I repent! Help me overcome my unrepentance!"

Application: Pick someone from Scripture who exhibits thoughtful and thorough repentance, and use them as a role model for future reference.

Supplication: Heavenly Father, please hear me, help me, and heal me. Where there is darkness, recall light. Where there is weakness, revive strength. Where there is wrong, restore right. Or wherever I should be, send me. Whatever I should do, tell me. Whenever I forget you, remind me. Please heap your mercies high for the sake of your Son, Jesus Christ. Come, Holy Spirit. Amen.

14

Holiness Prayer

You shall be holy, for I am holy.

1 Peter 1:16

Give us eyes to see
the gravity of our sin,
so we may know
the greatness of your love—
that forgiven much,
we shall love much more.

Sow in us
the seeds of holiness,
so we may bear
the fruits of love—
that dearer to you,
we are nearer to ourselves.

Set us apart, but not from each other:
that no one's righteousness
may be an island to another.

Better us, O Lord—
not that we may be admired—
but that you may be adored.

Forgive us, Father, for being
such a slow work of grace.
We are never clean till you cleanse us;
nor are we perfect till you perfect us.
You have said, "Be holy,"
so we pray—please hallow us.

In the name of the Father, the Son, and the Holy Spirit,
Amen.

Application: To adapt a line from Shakespeare, the course of true holiness never did run smooth. Fortunately, grace can make the whole process beautiful. To witness just such a transformation, watch the award-winning film *The Mission.*

Supplication: Lord, please teach me the true nature of holiness. Give me an accurate understanding that will translate into upright actions, actions that will solidify into honorable habits; habits that will grow into godly character; none of which, I understand, will get me into heaven, but all of which I hope will make you glad. Come, Holy Spirit. Amen.

15

Defining the Relationship

For now we see in a mirror dimly, but then face
to face. Now I know in part; then I shall know fully,
even as I have been fully known.

1 Corinthians 13:12

Some say that it's easy to have a personal relationship with
God. It's not. Eating a hot dog or drinking a beer is easy.
Knowing an invisible, ineffable, eternal, omniscient, omnip-
otent, omnipresent, triune deity is complicated! By all means
(or divine means), it's possible. But it's not happy-go-lucky. If
it were, those closest to God wouldn't often feel so far away.
But they do: everyone from Mother Teresa and Martin Luther,
to Job and Jesus Christ prayed, "My God, my God, why hast
thou forsaken me?" (Matthew 27:46 KJV).

A relationship with God is often uneasy and impersonal.
He gives us words to read, rather than His voice to hear. We

seek His counsel but receive His silence. We share ourselves with Him, but He remains a mystery to us. And if we count all our unanswered prayers and missing moments of intimacy, we'll be asking ourselves, "Do we really have a 'personal relationship'?"

The answer is no—we don't. What we have is personal and a relationship, but it's not like any other interpersonal relationship. Whereas two people become close by knowing one another, a Christian can be close to God without even knowing it. As Jesus indicated regarding the final judgment, many people will be considered righteous for having entertained God—not directly, but indirectly—by the kindness they've shown others, because our treatment of one another is a measurement of how we treat God. For some, this will be most serendipitous, but for others, it will prove catastrophic because as Jesus said, "Not everyone who says to me, 'Lord, Lord,' will enter the kingdom of heaven. ... And then will I declare to them, 'I never knew you'" (Matthew 7:21–23).

The extent to which we presently know God is less important than the extent to which He knows us. Distilled down, this life is for God to know us. The next life is for us to know Him. As Jesus said, "This is eternal life, that they know you the only true God" (John 17:3). This isn't to say God shouldn't be sought or to argue that He can't be found. But our expectations need to be altered. In this relationship, self-revelation extends both ways. It can occur when we lay open our lives by laying them down: feeding the hungry, forgiving the foe, and loving the neighbor. It can also happen when we continue to pray and study the Scriptures, even if it feels lifeless and insincere. And for all this, we might not experience anything, but God does. Because it's when God seems most absent to us, faithfulness can make us all the more present to Him.

Application: Great and enduring love relationships are based not just on feelings, but promises. Write down your vows to God and frame them.

Supplication: Lord, whatever my feelings of abandonment might be, may you never have to say of me, "My child, my child, why have you run away from me?" Nor let me forget, that should I never forsake you, it's only because you never forsook me. Come, Holy Spirit. Amen.

16

God and Gold

The Lord said to Moses: Tell the Israelites to
take for me an offering [of] ... gold, silver, [and]
bronze. ... And have them make me a sanctuary,
so that I may dwell among them.

Exodus 25:1–9

In the beginning, God asked men for gold. Not the other
way around. God asked, or rather, commanded, not once
or twice but forty-five times: His tabernacle had to have
"a mercy seat of pure gold ... a lampstand of pure gold ...
snuffers and trays of pure gold" (Exodus 37). Indeed, God's
tabernacle was El Dorado *à la Mount Sinai*.

So much gold gets us asking, "Is it too much gold?" Gilt
gives moderns guilt. Great cathedrals, ornate altars, and
sacred art arouse our righteous skepticism: we demur, much
like the disciples, "Why this waste? For this ... could have

been sold at a high price and the money given to the poor" (Matthew 26:9 NIV). It seems excessive, oppressive, and also unnecessary: why decorate without when the Holy Spirit lives within? And what good is a cathedral when Jesus says, "When you pray, go into your room and shut the door" (Matthew 6:6). Indeed, a lively conscience asks such questions; and an observant one quickly gets an answer. A worshiper should be wary of asking God for gold. But this does not answer why it was God who first asked the Israelites for gold.

God clearly doesn't need gold any more than He needs sacrifices. So perhaps the gold, or the beauty it represents, isn't for Him but for us. God's house, after all, is a mutual dwelling place. He allows it to be filled with beauty—in art, language, lighting, sound, décor, and design—in much the same way He lets us delight in the world's mountains, rivers, woods, and wildlife: that we may "shew forth thy praise" (Psalm 51:15 KJV).

Beauty can help lead us into God's presence. Its assistance, however, is complimentary, not compulsory. The human body is a home for the Holy Spirit with or without beauty's help. And yet, as Paul reminds us, "God arranged the members in the body, each one of them," so that one part cannot say to the other, "I have no need of you" (1 Corinthians 12). The head and the heart cannot say to the eyes and ears, or the imagination and aesthetic intuition, "I have no need of you." They belong to God—and the sublime beauty of a place can help return us to where we belong.

Application: Contemplate a sublime landscape painting, such as Tom Thompson's *Northern River*, J. M. W. Turner's *Sun Setting over a Lake*, or Ivan Shishkin's *In the Wild North*.

Supplication: Lord, my heart longs to take harbor in heaven. For the voyage, rig the mast of my mind with wonder, and fill the sails of my soul with delight. Let my ears take aboard the sounds of sublimity and anchor my eyes in the awareness of beauty. For as much as my soul longs to sail speedily from here to eternity, I know your instructions are to enjoy the journey as much as the arrival. Come, Holy Spirit. Amen.

17

With All Your Mind

And he said to him, "You shall love the Lord your God with all your heart and with all your soul and with all your mind. This is the great and first commandment."

Matthew 22:37–38

G od said to the high and low IQs alike, "You shall love the Lord your God ... with all your mind" (Matthew 22:37). Nobody, or rather, no mind is exempt. In theory, our first thoughts, like our first fruits, belong to God. In practice, however, holy thinking and holy learning are often wholly absent amongst our everyday priorities and practices.

Thomas à Kempis once wrote, "God will not ask us what books we have read, but what deeds we have done."[1] And he's right: we can't read our way into heaven; but we can and should read along the way. An open book, for instance, alongside an open mind and an open heart is an excellent way to get wisdom. And if we do not forsake the wisdom we have found, "She will protect you; love her, and she will watch over you" (Proverbs 4:6 NIV). But should someone think that wisdom cannot be found amongst worthwhile books, then perhaps they've never read one, and it's probably time they did.

Sacred reading isn't the only way to love the Lord with our entire mind, but it is an essential way. In fact, it's a doorway. It introduces us to better thinking and new thoughts (or old ones we need to re-remember). The Bible says, "Prepare your minds for action" (1 Peter 1:13 NASB), which we can do through daily reading, for ideas such as peacemaking in Bonhoeffer's *Life Together*, wonder in Annie Dillard's *Pilgrim at Tinker Creek*, charity in Kierkegaard's *Works of Love*, devotion in Thomas Merton's *No Man is an Island*, perfection in Thomas à Kempis's *The Imitation of Christ*, and heavenly longing in Augustine's *Confessions*—and, of course, the Bible above every other book!

By way of a biblical example, consider Paul. He wrote to Timothy from prison, "When you come, bring the cloak that I left … and also the books, and above all the parchments" (2 Timothy 4:13). Note, as Charles Spurgeon did, "Paul is inspired, and yet he wants books! He has been preaching at least for thirty years, and yet he wants books! He had seen the Lord, and yet he wants books! … He had been caught up into the third heaven, and had heard that which it was unlawful for a man to utter, yet he wants books! He had written the major part of the New Testament, and yet he wants books. … *You* [my congregation,] need to read."[2] So too, for us, we shouldn't just read Paul, but also read as Paul read.

Application: Create a reading schedule that allows you to complete six books in twelve months. For a list of suggestions, see the recommended reading list at the end of this book.

Supplication: Lord, help me to love You with my entire mind; to reason as well as I am able; to think as clearly as I am capable; to meditate as my mind was made to. When I'm ignorant, inform me; when I'm informed, enlighten me; when I'm enlightened, liberate me—because You promised that the truth shall set me free. Come, Holy Spirit. Amen.

18

Ask and Ye Shall Not Receive

When you ask, you do not receive,
because you ask with wrong motives.

James 4:3

Unanswered prayer is when we're most impatient with God. Like Job, we want answers. Preferably good ones! But our impatience—which is common to our condition—blinds us to God's uncommon patience. We may be the children of God—and thus deserving of our Father's attention—but our prayers are often far too childish: honest and earnest, but immature, unwise, and demanding. Saints are simply precocious, because as Paul reminds us, "We do not know what to pray for as we ought" (Romans 8:26).

Prayer is the most efficacious force in the world, which is why we use it for wrangling even the pettiest of personal gains. We try to bend divine means to selfish ends. We might pray such prayers unwittingly—and perhaps not for something so simple as a parking space at the mall—but all of us pray occasionally and earnestly for trivial, self-centered, and foolish things.

Fortunately, we're not alone in this. The disciples were just as guilty of saying the wrong things to Jesus. Peter, for instance, glorified Jesus in one verse, exclaiming, "You are the Christ" (Matthew 16:16), and a few verses later tried to dissuade Jesus from fulfilling His destiny in Jerusalem, to which Jesus had to reply, "Get behind me, Satan!" (Matthew 16:23). The saintly sons of Zebedee also misspoke, asking, "Lord, do you want us to tell fire to come down from heaven and consume them?" (Luke 9:54).

Unanswered prayer can be a mark of God's anger. But it is also proof of God's patience. Sometimes God treats our prayers as He does our sins: "He does not deal with us according to [them]" (Psalm 103:10). For if He did, God's outstretched hand might be a backhand, not an open one. But God's grace and love stays His stigmatic hands.

Fortunately, we do not pray into the ears of an angry God. Instead, we come before a praying God—because God is already praying for us through the intercession of Jesus Christ. The Lord is tirelessly promoting His generous plans for each of us: "plans to prosper you and not to harm you, plans to give you hope and a future" (Jeremiah 29:11 NIV). And not only is Jesus praying for us. The Holy Spirit is also praying with us: so that our requests will be answered in God, but even more importantly, so that God's prayers will be answered in us. For the greatest impediment to successful prayer is not when God says no to us; it's when we say no to God.

Application: When we say yes to God, God says yes to us all the more. Nowhere is this more beautifully illustrated than in Luke 1:26–56. Read this passage to be both edified and inspired.

Supplication: Lord, as much as I may pray, you pray more. So help me to care as much or more about your prayers, as mine. For as much as I want you to answer my prayers, it is a greater privilege to be an answer to yours. Come, Holy Spirit. Amen.

19

The Life and Death Zone

Who may ascend the mountain of the LORD?
Who may stand in his holy place?

Psalm 24:3

On May 26, 1953, Tom Bourdilon and Charles Evans attempted the final ascent of the world's highest mountain. The two mountaineers rose early and climbed far—making it within 300 feet of the summit—but they were forced to return by their malfunctioning oxygen equipment. They could have conquered the mountain, but they wouldn't have escaped the death zone. So the two climbers descended to safety and became the last men to almost be the first men to reach the top of the world. The very next day Edmund Hillary and Tenzing Norgay entered the history books when they successfully summited Mount Everest.

Just as a so-called death zone envelops the top of Everest—

an altitude at which the scarcity of oxygen cannot sustain human life—so too the heights of mystical experience that exist atop the mountain of the Lord seem inaccessible to all or most of us. There are some who make it to the top, like the mountaineers and mystics who tell us awesome tales, but most of us seem to have neither the ambition nor the ability to scale to such heights.

King David once asked, "Who may ascend the mountain of the LORD?" (Psalm 24:3 NIV). The Psalm responds, "The one who has clean hands and a pure heart" (v. 4 NIV). So perhaps this means none of us. Or maybe it's all of us. Paul wrote, "You were washed, you were sanctified, and you were justified … by the Spirit of our God" (1 Corinthians 6:11). The death zone is nothing, therefore, to she who has the Spirit of God. So just as Hillary and Norgay needed oxygen, which is the breath of life, to climb the world's tallest mountain, so we need the Holy Spirit, which is the breath of God, to ascend the mountain of the Lord.

The spiritual life is often charted as a series of peaks and valleys. Naturally, we prefer the ecstasies of the summit to the difficulties of the valley. But what if the Holy Spirit is more concerned with guiding our descent than with assisting our ascent? What if God doesn't want us atop His mountain? For the name of God is already honored on the mountaintops, which is why Jesus said, "Go into all the world and proclaim the gospel to the whole creation" (Mark 16:15). Go tell it on the river bend and the forest floor; go tell it amidst the weak and the strong, the rich and the poor. Go tell it in word and deed, because God is quickly found wherever He still needs to be known, which is in the world, not far above it.

Application: Whether you are ascending a mystical peak, or descending into a spiritual valley, one's soul must always subsist on the Holy Spirit. To this end, listen and pray along to the Taizé song, "Veni Sancte Spiritus." Translated, *veni sancte spiritus* means "come, Holy Spirit." Various versions of this song can be found online.

Supplication: Lord, you go where you go, regardless of me; and you do what you do, sometimes without me. But when you go where you go, bring me along. And when you do what you do, tell me too. Not so that you can serve me, but so that I can serve you. Come, Holy Spirit. Amen.

20

Question
and Answer

The Lord came and stood, calling. ...
"Samuel! Samuel!" And Samuel said,
"Speak, for your servant is listening."

1 Samuel 3:10

Wisdom often hides itself in questions rather than answers, and the world's wisest minds and methods ask accordingly. From Kant and quantum physics, to Socrates and the scientific method: progress is shaped like a question mark. And the same is often applied to prayer: ask correctly, "and it shall be given to you"; seek properly, "and you will find"; knock humbly, "and it will be opened to you" (Matthew 7:7). For if "you ask and do not receive, [it is] because you ask wrongly" (James 4:3).

This is often, however, the wrong paradigm for prayer. Granted, it's a part of it: petition, supplication, and inquiry are all important. But prayer, however pure, must extend beyond the art of acquisition and cross-examination, beyond appeals and attempts to get answers—because the central catalyst for spiritual progress isn't in God's answers, it's in His questions.

God often acts through the people He asks. When God wanted to establish His people in the Promised Land, He asked Abraham to "go from your country and your kindred … to the land that I will show you" (Genesis 12:1). Likewise, when God wanted Israel's attention, He began by talking to a single person. "And the LORD came and stood, calling as at other times, 'Samuel! Samuel!'" (1 Samuel 3:10). Often we think it works the other way around, as if we were talking to God first. But it's the opposite. God is ready and willing to act in wonderful ways, but He's waiting for us to take notice. He's asking us just as He asked Isaiah, "Whom shall I send, and who will go for us?" and hoping we will respond, "Here I am! Send me" (Isaiah 6:8).

But if we're honest, we're often afraid of where God will send us and what He might ask of us. Which is understandable. After all, who isn't a little scared that God might ask them to give away all their possessions or devote all their time to some dead-end cause? But just as Jesus said, "Ask anything in my name, [and] I will do it" (John 14:14), can we have enough faith to reply, "Ask anything in your name, and we will try"? Our hearts have hidden doors, and Jesus is at each one saying, "Here I am! I stand at the door and knock. If you hear my voice and open the door, I will come in" (Revelation 3:20 NLT). But Jesus knocks like He talks: with a still, small voice. Are we actually listening?

Application: Read and reflect on the parable of the two sons (Matthew 21:28–32).

Supplication: Speak, Lord, for your servant is listening. Speak kindly because your servant is faltering. But speak true, Lord, and see that what you say is what I do. Come, Holy Spirit. Amen.

21

Patient Trust

Be still before the LORD
and wait patiently for him.

Psalms 37:7

There are times in life when God's patience feels far more counterproductive and discouraging than efficacious or comforting. We would like God to quicken the pace of progress in our lives—whether it's to do with a professional matter, a personal relationship, or perhaps our future plans. Quite often, however, God seems more concerned with the quality of our "being" than the quickness of our "becoming."

God's patience is, paradoxically, at the heart of our impatience. The tension between God's timing and our limited tolerance for discomfort can be deeply frustrating. This frustration once inspired Teresa of Avila to complain to Jesus. It's said that Jesus replied, "Teresa, this is how I treat my friends," to which she responded, "No wonder you have so few friends." In such moments, however, prayer still remains

our best resort, and there's no better prayer than Pierre Teilhard de Chardin's:

> Above all, trust in the slow work of God.
> We are quite naturally impatient in everything
> to reach the end without delay.
> We should like to skip the intermediate stages.
> We are impatient of being on the way to something
> unknown, something new.
> And yet it is the law of all progress
> that it is made by passing through
> some stages of instability—
> and that it may take a very long time.
>
> And so I think it is with you;
> your ideas mature gradually—let them grow,
> let them shape themselves, without undue haste.
> Don't try to force them on,
> as though you could be today what time
> (that is to say, grace and circumstances
> acting on your own good will)
> will make of you tomorrow.
>
> Only God could say what this new spirit
> gradually forming within you will be.
> Give our Lord the benefit of believing
> that his hand is leading you,
> and accept the anxiety of feeling yourself
> in suspense and incomplete.[1]

Application: Progress requires perspective. Browse through some old photo albums or home movies and marvel at just how far you've come—or how far you've been brought.

Supplication: Lord, this life has its long struggles and its quick troubles. It's said that suffering produces endurance, which builds character, which also gives hopes. But if I'm being honest, I'd like you to just improve my situation or quickly improve me or just do both. But I suppose you'll do what's best, which is actually best for me. Come, Holy Spirit. Amen.

22

We Don't Need Miracles

Jesus said to [Thomas], "Have you believed
because you have seen me? Blessed are those
who have not seen and yet have believed."

John 20:29

God is not a hard master; but He is the master. He can
ask us to do anything or leave behind everything—fore-
going house and home, family and friends, jobs, plans and
lands. But God is also very generous. He gives us rewards for
what is His by rights. He says, "Everyone who has left [such
things] ... for my name's sake, will receive a hundredfold and
will inherit eternal life" (Matthew 19:29).

It is a handsome offer but an unsought honor. Quite
often we'd rather remain believers until we have to become
disciples. The submerged, often subconscious cost-benefit
analysis is that the price of belief is nothing, but the cost of

discipleship could be everything. Our preference is to be vol-*untold*, not to volunteer.

Paul said to hell (or heaven) with it: "I count everything as loss because of the surpassing worth of knowing Christ Jesus" (Philippians 3:8). He wants us to set our minds on things above, so we can freely give of ourselves here below. Paul believes nothing is lost if God is gained. He's so sure, he said, "I urge you [to] be imitators of me" (1 Corinthians 4:16). But if we're to be like Paul—who was once hardhearted Saul—then we too would like a miracle to help expedite our transformation. We want our own "Road to Damascus" miracle because nothing says this is the right thing to do like a big bright light and a voice from heaven. Quid pro quo— O Lord—if you give us a real, incontrovertible sign, we will give you whatever you ask for.

But perhaps we're mistaken. Our lives, after all, are "hidden with Christ in God" (Colossians 3:3). Because God chose to reveal Christ to posterity through the testimony of the Scriptures, it might be unnecessary for God to reveal Himself afresh every time we're wavering in our commitment. As Dietrich Bonhoeffer wrote, "There in the Scriptures is our life. ... It is not in our life that God's help and presence must still be proved, but rather God's presence and help have been demonstrated for us in the life of Jesus Christ."[1] But if the proof of Jesus Christ is insufficient, nothing will suffice. And if past miracles don't embolden us, present ones won't either. We will remain as we are, for what cannot be taken on faith will not be done in faith. As Jesus warned in the parable of the rich man and Lazarus, "If [people] do not hear Moses and the Prophets, neither will they be convinced if someone should rise from the dead" (Luke 16:31).

Application: Select one of Jesus' miracles and remind yourself throughout the day that this miracle actually happened.

Supplication: Lord, help me to see that blessed are they who believe without seeing. So don't give me signs when sincere faith will do. And don't check my wandering with wonder if simple trust will win me over. Please, just give me faith enough to believe in the God of miracles, with or without receiving one. Come, Holy Spirit. Amen.

23

Is God Your Real Father?

Yet, O LORD, you are our Father; we are the clay, and you are our potter; we are all the work of your hand.

Isaiah 64:8

A young man once spent Father's Day a long way from home, on an island in the Pacific Northwest. That morning, unable to telephone his father, he sat down and prayed for him near the shoreline of the Trincomali Channel. Time passed, and the young man's thoughts moved from one dad to another. He prayed that God would be even more a Father to him than his earthly father. As he prayed this, a prompting stirred within him. The man felt drawn to the Bible, and taking it in hand, the Scriptures fell open upon a certain page. As he looked down his eyes alighted on a single passage. It read, "I will be your Father, and you shall be my sons and daughters, says the LORD Almighty" (2 Corinthians 6:18 NLT).

The man could not believe his eyes, yet he trusted what they saw. He glimpsed that "Our Father which art in heaven" (Matthew 6:9 KJV) is also our Father here on earth. God's love makes short work of time and space. But still the young man prayed, "Holy Spirit, fill my heart with an even deeper experience of God's fatherhood, and an even greater knowledge of His love for me." For paternity is one thing, and intimacy is another. A child who is held in the arms of love knows more than their birth certificate could say. Yet despite the young man's prayers, nothing more happened.

There is a mystery in God's parenthood. The life of the world and all within it—past, present, and future—is held within the palm of God's hand, yet it seems so rare that we feel His touch. Must we wait till heaven for a hug and eternity for an embrace? Still, there are things the heart knows that the head forgets. The heart knows there is no tenderness more tender, no constancy more constant, no generosity more generous, or forgiveness more forgiving than God's. It knows that God is the Father who sent His only Son so that all children come home.

Home to what, exactly? Paul wrote, "No eye has seen, nor ear heard, nor the human heart conceived, what God has prepared for those who love him" (1 Corinthians 2:9 NRSV). So while we don't know what we're going home to, we do know to whom we're going home—even if God's fatherhood remains a mysterious experience at present. For the time being, however, God the Father has given us God the Son and God the Holy Spirit to help us—the children of God—to live this life together as the real (and imperfect) family of God.

Application: To develop closer bonds of intimacy and trust, when talking to God use the informal and affectionate name "Dad," rather than the formal and remote title of "Father."

Supplication: Heavenly Dad, you are my Father, and I am your child. How awesome is that! I cannot thank you enough, and thank you that you do not expect me to. Come, Holy Spirit. Amen.

24

All's Well That Ends Well

Do not be anxious about tomorrow,
for tomorrow will be anxious for itself.
Sufficient for the day is its own trouble.

Matthew 6:43

Jesus said, "Sufficient for the day is its own trouble" (Matthew 6:34). But many could scoff, *That's easy enough for a God-man to say*. Remove the hyphen and subtract the "God," and man's troubles quickly become more than sufficient. For we are not, as Dostoyevsky wrote, "creatures who can get used to anything."[1] We are creatures who are constantly worn down and worried because life is long and complex. It's busy, and it's expensive and demanding. But Jesus was not making an observation. He was making a promise: "Come unto me … and I will give you rest" (11:28).

The peace of Christ isn't found by looking for it but at

it. That is, as the old hymn goes, by "turning our eyes upon Jesus, [and] looking full on His wonderful face." Only then, do "the things of this world grow strangely dim, in the light of His glory and grace."[2] Similarly, His peace is lost when we look away from Him. When we fix our eyes upon our worries, it is the things of the next world that grow strangely dim. A sad fact, because, as C. S. Lewis said, "The Christians who did the most for the present world were precisely those who thought most of the next."[3]

Worry, if we let it, can become like atheism. It can grow into unbelief about *who* Jesus is and *what* Jesus says. This worry acts as if Jesus didn't exist; or that Jesus isn't who He says He is. But if we examine this worry, we'll discover that the reason Jesus isn't there isn't because He left, it's because He wasn't invited.

Peter recommends "casting all your anxieties on [Jesus], because he cares for you" (1 Peter 5:7). Likewise, Paul writes, "Do not be anxious about anything, but in everything by prayer and supplication with thanksgiving let your requests be made known to God" (Philippians 4:6). But if this is too much, we can simply pray, "I believe; help me in my unbelief!" (Mark 9:24). For whatever the occasion or extremity—minor or monumental—the love of God is ready to illuminate our darkness. God is like the sun, and we're the earth. God is always shining but not always seen because He waits for us to turn to Him, just as the dawn awaits the rotation of the earth.

In all things and by all means, we should cast our worries onto God. But even more, we should cast ourselves upon

God. For the heart of man belongs in the hands of God. Once it resides there, "All shall be well, and all manner of things shall be well."[4]

Application: Pray to God in whatever posture or capacity you feel most relaxed—taking a walk, having a bath, drinking a glass of wine, or whatever works for you—and invite Him into your rest and trust.

Supplication: Jesus, please be in me what you want me to be in you. For in order to be trusting, I need your trust. To be spiritual, I require your Spirit. And to be humble, I must have your humility. Because who am I without you? Or what can I accomplish apart from you? To be like you, Lord, I need you to be with me and in me too. Come, Holy Spirit. Amen.

25

The Sleeping God

> And a great windstorm arose, and the waves were
> breaking into the boat. ... But Jesus was in the stern,
> asleep on the cushion. And they woke him and said to
> him, "Teacher, do you not care that we are perishing?"
>
> *Mark 4:37–38*

Crisis and calamity call us back to God or at least cause us to call out to Him. Anxious billions have asked, "Where are you, God?" And He often seems far away. God is the Almighty Absentee, and His distance from our distress only compounds our concerns. Is He really unawake to our problems?

So imagine the disciples' alarm in finding Jesus near but asleep. "And they woke him, saying, 'Do you not care ...?'" (Mark 4:38). It's a valid question. They were in harm's way. Fear for one's life is a natural instinct. We all possess it. Only Jesus can say, "O ye of little faith" (Matthew 8:26 KJV). We cannot. In fact, we can sympathize with the disciples: it's one thing to walk on water when Jesus says, "Walk." It's another not to fear, when Jesus fails to say, "Do not be afraid."

Is Jesus unconcerned with our various anxieties? Definitely not, for the Bible says elsewhere, "Cast all your anxieties on him because he cares for you" (1 Peter 5:7 NIV). But why then is Jesus still asleep in the boat?

Perhaps it's because Jesus was awake in His final hours in the garden of Gethsemane. While the disciples rested, He sweated blood. Jesus slept when spiritual danger was far off, but was alert when it was close at hand. The disciples did the opposite. They feared physical dangers but were ignorant of spiritual hazards. Is it not telling that mere hours before Peter thrice denied Christ, Christ caught him asleep three times? Perhaps, like Peter, we're also awake when we needn't be and asleep when we shouldn't be.

God invites us to rest as He rests and to be vigilant as He is vigilant. "Do not fear [that which] can kill the body but cannot kill the soul" (Matthew 10:28). Instead, Jesus says, "Pray so that you will not fall into temptation" (26:41 NIV). But how can we resist temptation—especially its subtle and insidious forms—if we're neglectful of the spiritual reality that lies at the heart of human life? For if we're to live like Jesus, we must see that "we are not human beings having a spiritual experience" in this life; "we are spiritual beings having a human experience."[1] Which is to say, there is a lot more to us than we recognize, and life is much livelier than we realize. So we must abide evermore in Jesus Christ, for He alone, is "the way, the truth, and the life" (John 14:6).

Application: In times of both mortal and spiritual danger, the act of true faithfulness can sometimes seem terrible to endure, but also incredible to behold. For inspiration, watch the Grand Prix-winning film, *Of Gods and Men*.

Supplication: Jesus, I'm a lot like your disciples: I fret over my body but forget about my soul. Help me, instead, to live an integrated life of mind, body, and spirit. Showing as much concern (and common sense) for spiritual hazards as I should for physical dangers. Come, Holy Spirit. Amen.

26

Be Still
and Feel Nothing

And after the earthquake a fire,
but the LORD was not in the fire.
And after the fire the sound of a low whisper.

1 Kings 19:11–12

The world thinks we have to be on the move in order for something interesting to occur. Progress in life is measured by upward mobility. Human knowledge is constantly pursuing new horizons. Global travel is as sacrosanct as the medieval pilgrimage, and leisure is measured in degrees of velocity, altitude, and adrenaline. Contemporary life gets vertigo if it stands still. And while to the modern mind certain things may come to those who wait, it's only whatever's been left behind. But whether or not good things do come to those who wait, God does come to those who wait upon Him in stillness, silence, and expectancy. For it was in the quietude of Samuel's sleep that God called him three times. It was in the solitude of his study that Thomas Aquinas prayed through the logical complexities of the *Summa Theologica*. And it was in the solemnity of the Lord's Supper that C. S. Lewis received the idea of *The Screwtape Letters*.

Contrary to our expectations, amazing things can transpire in stillness. This is partly why Jesus said, "When you pray, go into your room and shut the door and pray to your Father who is in secret" (Matthew 6:6). Be still, because the greatest good of all—God—cannot be found, only received. Be still because the inverse is also true. As Blaise Pascal warned, "All human evil comes from a single cause, man's inability to sit still in a room."[1] For if the soul cannot be stilled—if it cannot rest in the highest good—it will find some lesser good, which would become a greater evil, since it will be a rival god.

If the world does prescribe stillness, it's to reconnect with oneself. As Socrates said, "Know thyself." But this is the world's wisdom, not God's. Instead, God says, "Be still, and know that I am God" (Psalm 46:10). Be still, not so you can find yourself or heed your inner voice—or even the voice of God—but rather so you can hear the quiet sound of God withdrawing the earthquake, the wind, and the fire. Be still in the silent assurance of God's whisper, which invites you to know God on the basis of what is already said about Him, rather than on further revelations of words and actions. Be still and learn to believe in God's presence with childlike faith—just as young children learn to believe in the permanence of objects:

that even if something is removed from their sight, it does in fact still exist. Indeed, be still—even if you see nothing, feel nothing, and doubt everything—because God does see, feel, and know everything. Be still because that should be enough.

Application: Take two minutes at the beginning, middle, and end of your day to become still and silent before God. Don't worry about attaining mystical perfection or acquiring anything from God. Just give Him the gift of your attention.

Supplication: Lord, show me what you showed Elijah: for you to proceed, everything else must recede. If need be, withdraw even your signs and wonders, so I may trust that in your apparent absence, I will still be able to enjoy your actual presence. Come, Holy Spirit. Amen.

27

From Time to Eternity

For everything there is a season,
and a time for every matter under heaven:
a time to be born, and a time to die.

Ecclesiastes 3:1–2

The greatest surprise parties—or the worst—are funerals. When the dead die, they leave the living in the lurch, caught flatfooted by the foiled hope that there remained more time. But as Samuel Johnson once wrote, "Nothing is more evident than that ... age must terminate in death. ... The last year, the last day must come."[1] The sudden finality of such occasions often catches the survivors off guard, even if they're prepared, but death shouldn't come as a surprise for the dying. Life has left us all well warned.

Christ has overcome the power of death, but He hasn't removed its presence. Since our supernatural life still has to pass through our natural death, we should prepare ourselves—not for what comes next—but how we will face it.

C. S. Lewis has a quote from *King Lear* written on his tombstone: "Men must endure their going hence."[2] While talking about death is admittedly morbid, if we're silent on the subject, we can't really talk about life—not real life. It would stop us from declaring that Jesus is the way, the truth, and the life because we wouldn't have a way to talk truthfully about life. And truth be told, if we can't be reconciled with reality, we have no business reconciling others with Christ.

The awareness that life ends can add to the appreciation of it. This is because death can shine a light as much as it can cast a shadow. It can show us that however lengthy life may be, it's not long till it is over, so it should be lived with wonder and courage—for the goodness of life merits the former, and the nature of it requires the latter. It reveals—much like a loved one who cannot stay for long or an old friend who's only visiting—that the knowledge of a departure adds to the appreciation of the stay.

There is a Latin maxim, *Memento mori*, which reminds its hearers that earthly existence has an expiry date. It has long served the Christian tradition as an encouragement to live not just a full life but also a good one. As Thomas à Kempis wrote, "Wise and blessed is he who, during life, strives to be what he would like to be when death finds him."[3] But this focus on death isn't meant to scare us into living a rigidly moral life. Instead, it's God's way of reminding us to deliberately choose a real and rewarding life. A life that will stretch on into eternity, alive and pulsing like never before, progressing like the steps of a dance from glory to glory.

Application: In classical music, the Requiem Mass marks death by celebrating both life and the life hereafter. Through the grace of music, death is transfigured into beauty. Get comfortable on a couch or in bed, and listen to Mozart's *Requiem Mass*, Fauré's *Requiem*, or Brahms' *A German Requiem*.

Supplication: Jesus, whether my duration here is long and easy or short and hard; whether my departure is brief and blessed or tortuous and torturous—help me to make good my going hence. Come, Holy Spirit. Amen.

28

Supernatural Selection

And they went with haste and found Mary and Joseph,
and the baby lying in a manger.

Luke 2:16

We reenact the nativity more regularly than we realize.
At Christmas, we do so literally or at least the kids do:
every character identically arrayed in their parent's bathrobe.
But in a larger sense, we're engaged in reenactment whenever
we embark on Christian work. Christ's nativity and Christian
ministry are much alike.

Christ was born in a stable among animals, manure, and
simple people. Only God could extract glory from some-
where so unglamorous and unlikely. In fact, it seems to be His
preferred mode of operation. Christian undertakings rarely
commence under ideal conditions: the ministry of Francis
began in a broken-down church, and the great Pentecostal

Azusa Street Revival originated in a warehouse. God gives us classrooms, street corners, and empty garages and asks us to turn them into sanctuaries. We may prefer Jerusalem-like places: an attractive church, a fancy boardroom, a lively recreation center, or perhaps a chic café, but God gives us Bethlehems and Nazareths. If we waited for what looked right, we'd seldom begin, but God asks us to make do. We often reply, like Nathanael, *Can anything good come from a place like Nazareth?* God says, *Come and see.*

Christian ministry and Christ's nativity are also similarly stuffed with unqualified people. The facts of Jesus' birth point to this: nobody knew what they were doing. The shepherds were unscheduled. The magi arrived late. Mary didn't know how to mother God, and Joseph was lousy at logistics. Their sole qualification was the help of the Holy Spirit, which is as true today as it was two thousand years ago. For whatever expertise or experience we may possess—individually or collectively—it is only by the power of God that our fumbling efforts can be transformed into something redemptive and beautiful. This is the only power worth praying for.

Christ's nativity and Christian ministry are also both by invitation only. "No one can come to me unless the Father who sent me draws them" (John 6:44 NIV). Neither the wise men's wisdom nor the shepherds' simplicity won them their invitation. They were there by God's welcome. So too, for us: it is neither "this man's art nor that man's scope"[1] that ordains them into the priesthood of all believers. It is the unmerited generosity and grace of God.

Application: Whenever you next engage in ministry, remember that whatever your strengths or weaknesses, nobody has earned the right to do God's work but instead has been graciously invited.

Supplication: Lord, though I minister, it's still your ministry. So blaze the trail you wish me to tread and be the power I'm powerless without. In all I am, in all I do, be my all in all. For it's not my place to invite you into my ministry, but to be invited into yours. Come, Holy Spirit. Amen.

29

More Love

You shall love your neighbor as yourself.

Mark 12:31

The Golden Rule is both a cornerstone and a stumbling block. Its importance is obvious, as are our failures: we neither love our neighbors as ourselves, nor ourselves as we should. Yet we must. It is the Golden Rule, not the gilded suggestion. And it's worth noting that the command is to love our neighbor *as* ourselves and not *instead of* ourselves. We owe ourselves a large debt of love. But talking about it, let alone paying it, makes some people feel uneasy. They would rather neglect the self than risk indulging it. Yet, as C. S. Lewis wrote, "It would be a horrible command if the self were simply to be hated."[1] And as Paul reminds us, "No one ever hated his own flesh, but nourishes and cherishes it" (Ephesians 5:29).

Self-love is not the same as self-lust. Self-lust exists for self-fulfillment, self-love longs for soul-fulfillment. It yearns for the soul to be united with God. It cries out, as Augustine did, "You have made us for yourself, O Lord, and our heart is restless until it rests in you."[2] Self-love is also not to be mistaken with those who in the last days, as the Bible warns, "will be lovers of self" (2 Timothy 3:2). Instead, self-love ennobles, not indulges, the self. It says, like Paul, "I discipline my body and keep it under control, lest after preaching to others I myself should be disqualified" (1 Corinthians 9:27).

Self-love gives to itself in order to give of itself. It honors itself with time to pray and study; it accepts silence and solitude; and it welcomes rest and reflection. In a word, self-love invests in itself by being disciplined about the spiritual disciplines. And it does so, because it has to be. The pace and priorities of normal life are inhospitable to the spiritual life and, at times, openly hostile because the prioritization of our spiritual life can seem selfish or insulting to whoever or whatever wants our attention.

The degree to which we love ourselves—which is measured by how we assist or inhibit our own efforts to be in relationship with God—is indicative of how well we will love our neighbors. For if we can't even love ourselves properly—for which we have every reason to do so—what hope is there for loving others? But since we're all guilty of favoring our own wants above others' needs, it's clear that we're struggling to love our neighbors as we should and ourselves as we ought. But we could better our love, God willing, if we attempted something bold. If we chose to only love ourselves as much as we love our neighbors, we would quickly learn what is required to love our neighbors as ourselves.

Application: Schedule for yourself a soul-care day. Likewise, find a way to concretely contribute toward someone else's welfare.

Supplication: Heavenly Father, help me to love my neighbor no less than myself; myself no more than my neighbor; and yourself above both my neighbor and myself. Come, Holy Spirit. Amen.

30

How Much Should I Give? A Prayer

It is more blessed to give than to receive.

Acts 20:35

Heavenly Father,
the love of money may produce
all kinds of evil, but the command to give
also creates its own kind of concerns.

The Old Testament tells of tithing 10 percent,
but Zacchaeus gave half and recompensed more.
In Jerusalem the Church held everything in common,
and Ananias and Sapphira died for not doing more.

But is it right to give alms with arms wide open,
when the just consider both merit and need,
the wise measure intentions against outcomes,
and the prudent balance both giving and saving?

Paul wrote that whoever sows sparingly,
or bountifully, shall reap accordingly.

He also said a man must give as his heart has chosen—
cheerfully, not reluctantly, or under compulsion.

Part of me asks, *How little is too little?*
Another, *How much is too much?*
A third part is obliging but complacent,
and thinks, *Enough is enough*.

A last part prays (and this is my prayer):
whatever you require, whenever you desire—
whatsoever my reluctance—help me to give, Lord,
because you're enough for me.

Amen.

Application: In the Bible, Paul says to give what you have in mind to give and to give it with good cheer. If you are willing, however, ask what God has in mind for you to give, and then give it in good faith.

Supplication: Lord, should I forget that it's just as wrong to keep my money at another's expense, as it is to make it—caution me. Should I show as much love for money through its retention as its acquisition—correct me. I hope, however, that as much as I may secretly love money, or the things it can buy, I will sincerely love You even more. But if this isn't so, please make it so. Come, Holy Spirit. Amen.

31

The S Word

Now I rejoice in my sufferings …
filling up what is lacking in Christ's afflictions,
for the sake of … the church.

Colossians 1:24

It is considered a mark of maturity to endure the company of the unwanted, to abide the annoying, and to bear the unbearable. And so it is, but this is not yet Christian maturity. A Christian is not merely to suffer another but for another. This is love. And love's call has an echo—suffering.

In a manner of speaking, Christ did not come to reduce our suffering so much as He came to save us from the kind of suffering that reduces us to nothing. In fact, Christ came to transform both the quality and the purpose of our suffering. As Peter wrote, "Christ … suffered for you, leaving you an example, so that you might follow in his steps" (1 Peter 2:21). And the footsteps of Christ are an exercise in love. Suffering is but love's sweat. But unlike in physical exercise, where we expect to perspire, when our neighborly love becomes too difficult, we disengage. Too much exertion seems unpleasant, costly, even surprising. But it is important. In negative terms, to suffer for another is to incur the costs of being virtuous. But put positively, it's a capital investment in the life of another.

The Bible says, "Provided we suffer with [Jesus] … we may also be glorified with him" (Romans 8:17). And to top it off, one is meant to rejoice "in so far as you share in Christ's sufferings" (1 Peter 4:13). Clearly, perfection for heaven is psychosis to the world. After all, who likes suffering? And who's back is broad enough for more than one cross? Indeed, do we give gladly? Do we speak warmly? Do we pray fervently, not to share someone's burden, but to avoid it? Yet, Paul rejoices in suffering, "filling up what is lacking in Christ's afflictions" (Colossians 1:24). But what could be lacking when it comes to Christ?

Perhaps what's lacking isn't Christ's afflictions but Christ in us. After all, every Christian is to be like Christ to her neighbor: to love as loved, to give as given, to forgive as forgiven, and, if need be, to suffer as suffered for. This is the work that needs to be done because there are always unglamorous glories to be won. But even if the life of a Christian, which is the life of Christ, can sometimes be unpleasant and painful, we can still be at peace. As the Bible promises, "After you have suffered [only] a little while, the God of all grace, who has called you to his eternal glory in Christ, will himself restore, confirm, strengthen, and establish you" (1 Peter 5:10).

Application: Talk to someone you admire, such as a teacher, parent, or pastor, about how they developed greater forbearance, self-sacrifice, and love.

Supplication: Lord, in order to give more of me, I need more of you. For when your love abides, my love abounds. Indeed, give me love enough to suffer, because you've suffered enough for love. Thank you. Come, Holy Spirit. Amen.

32

A Shekel for Your Thoughts

Knowledge puffs up, but love builds up.

1 Corinthians 8:1

The Christian tradition recognizes two sets of virtues. The first are the theological virtues of faith, hope, and love. The second are called cardinal virtues, which consist of wisdom, justice, temperance, and courage. Tradition sets no limit on how much faith, hope, and love we can have, but the cardinal virtues have always come with a caveat. Too much of a good thing is a bad thing: excessive courage is recklessness; strait justice forgets mercy; and too much temperance is too little fun. As for wisdom, the Bible says, "[With] much wisdom is much vexation, and he who increases knowledge increases sorrow" (Ecclesiastes 1:18). It would be prudent, therefore, regarding the acquisition of wisdom, to ask just how much of our religious learning is really helpful.

Lord Byron famously warned, "The tree of knowledge is not the tree of life."[1] If religious knowledge becomes the primary focus of our religion, the purity of our thoughts will not compensate for the impurity of our hearts. As Thomas Merton rightly attests, "The whole problem of our time is not lack of knowledge but lack of love."[2] There is a problem if we are more concerned with good books than good deeds. There is a discrepancy if we talk more *about* God than *to* God. And we're in danger if we think that theological learning is in itself an act of worship, because people can seek and love the truth for all the wrong reasons.

The degree to which our religious learning helps us to ultimately fulfill the first two commandments is the same degree to which it is beneficial for us. Knowledge is meant to serve us so we can serve others, which is why Paul says, "Whatever is true, whatever is honorable, whatever is just, whatever is pure, [and] whatever is lovely, ... think about these things" (Philippians 4:8). Think on them because love is an act of the will, which has to take root in the mind if it is to last in the heart. Think on them because the heart cannot be reformed without being, "transformed by the renewal of our minds" (Romans 12:2). For without the renewal of the mind, we cannot "discern what is the will of God, what is good and acceptable and perfect" (Romans 12:2). But this renewal cannot be achieved through our own strength, since the mind cannot be wholly (or holy) transformed by the power of its own thoughts. Instead, each of us requires the ministry of the Holy Spirit, who graciously initiates, expedites, and rewards our studies with the gift of true knowledge, which is slowly obtained through our advancement in the prerequisites of learning, which are humility, patience, hard work, and prayer.

Application: Develop the habit of praying before you read or study, asking for the opportunity to bless others with what you will learn.

Supplication: Lord, my prayer is to know what I love and to love what I know. It's also to love with what I know and to know that I do love. Come, Holy Spirit. Amen.

33

The Wrong Question

He said to him …, "Simon, son of John, do you
love me?" Peter was grieved … and he said to him,
"Lord, you know everything; you know that
I love you." Jesus said to him, "Feed my sheep."

John 21:17

Dmitri grew up as a sheltered, earnest, and high-minded
boy. Since leaving home, he's become a successful man:
quick-witted, well liked, thoroughly traveled, and profes-
sionally accomplished. But while Dmitri's achievements are
prodigious, his lifestyle is prodigal. He is lecherous, unkind,
an alcoholic, and verging on apostate. He's lost his way, his
religion, and himself. And he often loses sleep, lying awake,
lonely and worried, working over a single, simple, searing
question: does Jesus love me?

The answer to Dmitri's question—but not the question
itself—is hugely important. Of course, Jesus loves him. It's

Bible Basics 101. "God shows his love for us in that while we were still sinners, Christ died for us" (Romans 5:8). Christ's grace is for the ungracious, His faith for the faithless, and His love for the unlovable. Jesus says, "It is not the healthy who need a doctor, but the sick. I have not come to call the righteous, but sinners" (Mark 2:17 NIV). But not everyone is convinced, because many of us still pray, "Jesus, do you love me?" And like Dmitri, we're asking the wrong question because it's not so much ours to ask but to answer.

Consider the case of Peter. He and Jesus had the most unique friendship in history: they did everything together from walking on water to changing the world. But Peter, as if to prove Oscar Wilde right—that a true friend stabs you in the front—denied even knowing Christ. He betrayed Jesus in a way Judas never could. But afterward Peter never had to ask, *Jesus, do you love me?* He knew Jesus well enough. Instead, Jesus asked Peter, "Do you love me?" (John 21:15–17). Because it was Peter who needed to hear his own answer before he could resume the leadership of Jesus' flock.

Jesus also asks each of us, "Do you love me?" If the answer is yes, we are meant to return to our shepherd. "[For] we all, like sheep, have gone astray" (Isaiah 53:6 NIV). But for some of us, it's the return journey that proves to be the path of greatest resistance, because we're afraid to reform old habits. So we ask the do-you-love-me question in order to shift the focus away from our shortcomings, since it's easier to be loved than to love, just as it's harder to give than to receive. So like Dmitri, we ask the wrong question because we're afraid of the right answer. We prefer to play the shepherd not the sheep: to be followed around by Jesus rather than to follow.

Application: Everyone in creation is a unique being. So reflect on how you can uniquely love Jesus.

Supplication: Jesus, my heart should long to love you as much as it wants to be loved by you. Yet sin lurks where love should live. So let me see how far I've fallen, so I'll know how high you'll raise me. Because forgiven much, I'll love you that much more. Come, Holy Spirit. Amen.

34

Help Me to Love: A Prayer

Love bears all things, believes all things, hopes all
things, endures all things. Love never ends.

1 Corinthians 13:7–8

Plant in me a love
that believes everything believable,
and then nurture it with your belief,
which believes the unbelievable.

Water within me a love
that hopes in the hopeful,
and then freshen it with your hope,
which hopes even in the hopeless.

Shine within me a love
that endures all things,
and enlighten it with your endurance,
which endures the unendurable.

And prune in me a love
that cares unceasingly,
and tend it with Your timelessness,
which has no end or beginning.

Then gather from me the fruits of affection,
which include kindness, patience, and protection.

Pick from me the flowers of care,
which are free from pride and full of prayer.

Arrange from me a garland of grace,
which does not boast, begrudge, or debase.

And weave from me a wreath of amity,
which is woven with faith, hope, and charity.

Amen.

Application: Love without action devolves from goodwill into good intentions. Love someone today by showing them kindness or generosity.

Supplication: I don't need to radically love, if I simply love, because love by itself is radical enough. So help me just to love. Come, Holy Spirit. Amen.

35

The Forgettable God

Remember these things, O Jacob, and Israel …;
I formed you; you are my servant;
O Israel, you will not be forgotten by me.

Isaiah 44:21

January and February are the worst months in winter. In this period, the weather becomes very wearisome. Villages like Snag in Canada's Yukon can experience temperatures as cold as -63 °C (-81 °F), and towns like Barrow, Alaska, endure up to sixty-seven days of continuous night. It's not uncommon to experience melancholia or worse—seasonal affective disorder. But apart from medical treatment and light therapy, the best one can do is remember that winter is a temporary and disorienting time but over soon.

Memory can also have a fortifying effect in our spiritual winters. When we remember the words of Scripture—to be strong and courageous because the Lord will not leave or forsake us (Deuteronomy 31:6)—we reopen ourselves to the Spirit behind the Scriptures. But forgetfulness is one of our reoccurring flaws. In fact, the greatest challenge of the Old Testament wasn't about believing in God; it was remembering Him. There was no shortage of miracles and revelations, only recollection. Hence the frequent exhortations to remember, such as, "You shall remember … the LORD your God who brought you out from [Egypt]" (Deuteronomy 5:15). Indeed, we must remember, because faith is impossible without a long memory.

Memory is vital to devotion because it is central to relationship. In a marriage, for instance, one must remember their vows in hard times in order to reach better times. Likewise, one must remember to trust in the love of their partner without the need of endless reaffirmation; because the more they accept the reality of their partner's love, the deeper their own love will become. So too, in spiritual terms, we should try to remember the goodness of God rather than asking God to repeatedly demonstrate it. A relationship is built on acts of trust just as much as acts of love.

The famous philosopher Søren Kierkegaard experienced more misfortune and grief than most, but in some of his last written words, he wrote that every single individual is equally close to God because God equally loves each of us. "If there is any [inequality]," Kierkegaard wrote, "it is that one person bears in mind that he is loved … and can go through life … meditating on how he is loved … [and] another person does not remember that he is loved."[1] The difference is one discovered the greatest truth in the universe and remembered it, and the other did not.

Application: Important truths can be represented in a variety of ways. Find a piece of poetry, music, or art that you can use as a daily reminder that God loves you.

Supplication: Lord, help me not to forget You, because You never forget me. Thank You that You love me, and may this be a reminder to also love You. Come, Holy Spirit. Amen.

36

Is God Your Friend?

I have called you friends …

John 15:15

We often apprehend God's love for us as that of a Father for lost children, a King for His kingdom, and a Creator for His creation. While each of these apprehensions is accurate, there's still more to His love because Jesus feels for us the fondness of friendship. In John's gospel, Jesus said to His disciples, "I have called you friends" (15:15). Not followers or worshipers but friends: the people He preferred to eat with, joke with, and walk with through Galilee. He even died for them, telling them, "Greater love has no one than this: to lay down one's life for one's friends" (John 15:13 NIV).

The fact that Jesus died for His friends—past, present, and future—testifies to the vitality and validity of the famous hymnal refrain "What a friend we have in Jesus."[1] But the more we think about it, the more it begs the question, what kind of a friend is Jesus?

Both modern and ancient wisdom recognize multiple forms of friendship. Aristotle, for instance, identified friendships of utility (e.g. business partners), inequality (e.g. between parents and children), and equality (in which peers selflessly seek each other's good). In our own experiences, many of us have probably faced imbalanced forms of friendship. Perhaps it's a friend who enjoys helping but not being helped; maybe they always talk but rarely listen; or they like to open people up but personally remain closed off.

So what kind of a friend is Jesus? Is He always giving and never receiving? Is our friendship based on utility or inequality? Or is our friendship founded on equality, symmetry, and mutual care?

The story of Simon of Cyrene and how he helped carry Jesus' cross suggests that Jesus is a true friend to us, because He accepts true friendship from us (whether, like Simon, we realize it at the time or not). For it was during the passion of Christ—the very climax of His incarnation—that Jesus was so humble as to be helped by someone He was helping; to be supported by someone He was saving; and to share the weight of the cross, which held the weight of all our sins. Indeed, what a friend we have in Jesus. Despite the inequality between His divinity and our humanity, He welcomed people like us as friends on the road to Calvary. And what a kingdom to which we belong—a kingdom of friends—where no one has to carry their cross alone, not even Jesus Christ.

Application: The next time you are hanging out with your best friend, pray that Jesus will be welcome amidst your fellowship.

Supplication: Jesus, thank you for the gift of true friendship! Let our bond become bounded by joy, adventure, loyalty, and love. I know I can't be as good a friend to you, as you are to me, but help me to be the best kind of friend to you that I can be. Come, Holy Spirit. Amen.

37

Suffering Servants

Out of the anguish of his soul
he shall see and be satisfied.

Isaiah 53:11

The book of Isaiah speaks eloquently and mournfully of a suffering servant: "Surely he has borne our griefs and carried our sorrows; yet we esteem him stricken, smitten by God, and afflicted" (53:4). The anonymous identity of this servant was revealed in a man known by many names: עוֹשִׁי, Χριστός, and Jesus. But the role of the suffering servant is replayed around the world by countless others. There are everyday servants such as Maria and Father Babu. In one, the suffering servant is recast as a young woman who loves a city's down-and-outs by living with them; the other is a priest who lives in a foreign land, accepting loneliness so others can enjoy his undivided attention.

A suffering servant reminds us that a crown of glory begins as one of thorns. The yoke is easy and the burden light, but as Shakespeare illustrated, "Uneasy lies the head that wears a crown."[1] It is heavy with responsibility and care. Do we still want to take the coronation oath? And do we answer, "We will," when Jesus asks, "Are you able to drink the cup that I drink, or to be baptized with the baptism with which I am baptized?" (Mark 10:38).

Paul wrote, "Provided we suffer with him … we may also be glorified with him" (Romans 8:17). The command, however, isn't to suffer but to love. But the difficulty with love—and hence the suffering—is that love usually comes at the expense of the lover. Because the greatest gift we have to give is also the only gift we can give, which is ourselves. And we know this to be true in relationships, marriages, and families but also with respect to our lesser loves and longings. We know that we have to give of ourselves to get the things that we deeply desire like top grades, good physiques, and professional accomplishments. We willingly suffer the loss of our time, energy, and resources for these lesser loves, and both the bags under our eyes and the awards on our walls attest to it.

Likewise, if we love God with any degree of intensity, the scars of that love will soon show. The marks of suffering will begin to appear in the company we keep, the budgets we make, and the schedules we create. But just as there is much to give, so there is much to gain. For one thing, as the Bible promises, "Suffering produces endurance, and endurance produces character, and character produces hope, and hope does not put us to shame" (Romans 5:3–5).

Application: How you spend your time is how you live your life. List the five things that matter most to you and order them according to how much time, energy, and effort you invest into each of them.

Supplication: Lord, take not my best but my all. My time is yours to use. My money is yours to spend. Even my life—if necessary—is yours to lose. For who I am, is safe in whom I trust. Come, Holy Spirit. Amen.

38

To Boldly Love:
A Prayer

But I say to you who hear, Love your enemies, do good
to those who hate you, bless those who curse you, pray
for those who abuse you. To one who strikes you on the
cheek, offer the other also, and from one who takes away
your cloak do not withhold your tunic either. Give to
everyone who begs from you, and from one who takes
away your goods do not demand them back. And as you
wish that others would do to you, do so to them.

Luke 6:27–31

Let us not be afraid, O Lord,
to give away what we love,
to the people you love;
and giving for you,
may we receive
more of you.
Amen.

Application: To give away what you like is generosity. To give away what you love is a sacrifice. Neither form of giving comes easily, but to see how much good can be done when we are willing to give with an open heart, watch the movie *Schindler's List*.

Supplication: God, grant me the grace to be as willing to give, as I am to receive. Come, Holy Spirit. Amen.

39

The End of the World

But concerning that day and hour
no one knows, not even the angels of heaven,
nor the Son, but the Father only.

Matthew 24:36

In the year 1666, the world appeared to be ending, not with a whimper but with a very definite bang—at least for Britain. In this *annus horribillis*, the English suffered a stunning naval defeat in the North Sea, the Great Plague stalked its cities, and the Great Fire of London consumed its capital. These events left England weary and wary, wondering what evil might come next. In the minds of many, these disasters suggested that the end of the world was near—especially since the year 1(666) supposedly contained the biblical sign for the approaching Apocalypse.

Three hundred and fifty years later, we still have eschatological extremists: Y2K hysterics, Mayan 2012 prophets, and religious nuts who pull their kids out of school because the end is nigh. In another 350 years, there will probably be just as many or more. But it is true that the world occasionally catches fire—as in 1666—which forces all of us to look for meaning in seemingly impossible situations.

In 1666, when England was ablaze, one young man resisted the urge to ignore either his everyday obligations or his lifelong aspirations. The young scholar dutifully continued his studies in the countryside, away from Cambridge and the plague, and in the process invented calculus, revolutionized the study of optics, and discovered the law of universal gravitation. He was Sir Isaac Newton. And while none of us can rival his accomplishments, we can all emulate his attitude because he rightly recognized that the most important things in life are rarely to be postponed.

C. S. Lewis once told his students during wartime, "If men had postponed the search for knowledge and beauty until they were secure the search would never have begun."[1] So too, in periods of great calamity—like wars, epidemics, and natural disasters—the best of humanity remains committed to life even in the worst of times. They understand that the life of the world is not saved by abandoning it or by remaining aloof from it, but only by entering deeper into it. Likewise, we are indebted to those brave souls who have suffered personal misfortunes and still kept faith with a world that felt all but lost:

like Beethoven, who was deaf when he composed the Ninth Symphony, and John Milton, who was blind when he wrote *Paradise Lost*. Their lesson for each of us is that the doors of life are always open, and we can go about important business—just as Jesus went about God's business—regardless of whether it's the world's first day or seems like it's the last.

Application: Create a personal motto that you can recite whenever life seems hardest, or about to end.

Supplication: Lord, if the world is ending—or my life within it—keep the light of faith, hope, and love alive and flickering. Come, Holy Spirit. Amen.

Don't Believe in God

And stretching out his hand toward his disciples,
he said, "Here are my mother and my brothers!
For whoever does the will of my Father in heaven
is my brother and sister and mother.

Matthew 12:49–50

If you've been told that the single most important thing in
life is to believe in Jesus Christ, someone has misled you.
This is not God's greatest concern. It is merely a necessary—
but by itself insufficient—part of a much more extensive
plan for you. However, there is a tendency in some circles to
over emphasize the importance of believing in Jesus Christ.
It's as if we've got hung up on the opening notes of a piece
of music—like the first four notes of Beethoven's Fifth Symphony (short-short-short-long), and we can't remember the
rest of the song. But the main motif can never be a substitute
for the rest of the symphony, just as our faith in Jesus isn't a
replacement for the rest of Christianity.

The importance of belief should not be underestimated because it is true "if you confess with your mouth that Jesus is Lord and believe in your heart that God has raised him from the dead, you will be saved" (Romans 10:9). But as correct as it is to stress that belief is at the heart of being born again, it's wrong to think that it's the totality of what God has intended for our lives. Simply put, God doesn't just want us to be born again; He wants us to grow up. Jesus didn't come to make infantile believers but adult family members. And though the process of adoption begins with belief, we can only come of age through discipleship. We may need childlike faith, but we were never meant to be forever young.

Jesus declared, "All people will know you are my disciples, if you have love for one another" (John 13:35). He said this because He wanted the family of God to be primarily known—not by a common belief but by an uncommon love. Jesus is dying (or died) to be known by His love for us, by our love for Him, and our love for one another.

In the Great Commission, Jesus said, "Go therefore and make disciples of all nations" (Matthew 28:19). Notice that Jesus asked for disciples and not believers, because it's possible to believe in Jesus without being His disciple. But it's impossible to be a disciple of Jesus and not believe in Him. We can mentally assent to every doctrine about the divinity of Christ without actually lifting a finger for the benefit of another, but to be a disciple requires much more. In fact, a life of discipleship is the greatest and most demanding adventure in the world. God wants to know, are we ready?

Application: Jesus sent out His disciples in pairs. Find a partner who will pray and join with you in the great adventure that lies ahead.

Supplication: Jesus, I never want to worship or believe in anybody or anything but you. What I also want—but seldom do—is to not live any way other than you, nor love any less than you do. So, naturally—or supernaturally—I need less of me and more of you. Come, Holy Spirit. Amen.

Conclusion

The things, good Lord, that we pray for,
give us the grace to labor for.

Saint Thomas More, The Oxford Book of Prayer [1]

This conclusion was very nearly excised. Because the longer an author writes, or just this author, the more apparent the law of diminishing returns becomes. Regardless of whether the chapter titles vary, or the words on each page dance a little differently, when the message does not change, it's time for the messenger to end the message. For how many times can I extoll the primacy of love without becoming a pain in the neck? Or prescribe faithfulness and not become patronizing? If I have spoken too much on particular topics, such as the burdens of blessings, the importance of impious honesty, God's grace for the ungracious, and the need for charity to circumvent uncharitable feelings, then please forgive me, and thank you for bearing with me.

Wherever possible I have pluralized my observations and exhortations, choosing "we" over "you," to avoid making the impression in your head or my heart that the author has acquired any degree of sanctity. This book was in fact written for my own benefit, as it was inspired by my own shortcomings. So I freely confess, in the words of T. S. Eliot, "Between the idea / and the reality / between the motion / and the act / falls the shadow."[2]

Indeed, this book emerged from the shadows of a very difficult season in my life. The last four years have been my winter with God. Through it, I have seen my prospects fall like snow from very high places to very low ones. I have watched cherished dreams vanish before my eyes, like the vapor of one's breath on a cold day. And for a time, everyone and everything I held dear was stripped from me, like the leaves off a tree just before winter. It has not been easy. I am often afraid of how long this season might last. But then there are occasional moments of clarity when I hope this winter will last forever. Because hardship has turned my eyes to God and helped me to see, when I have had nowhere else to look, that every good and perfect gift does in fact come from above (James 1:17). In the absences of winter—of warmth, light, and life—I've finally felt the incontrovertible presence of God's consuming fire and encompassing love. In the end, winter with God became life with God. So perhaps, in retrospect, Shakespeare's *Richard III* should say that now is the winter of our contentment. Now is the season of life, growth, and luminosity.

WINTER WITH GOD:
A Reading List

> I heard a voice from the nearby house chanting
> as if it might be a boy or girl (I do not know which),
> saying and repeating over and over again,
> "Pick up and read, pick up and read."
>
> *St. Augustine, Confessions*[1]

A good book should always lead its reader to another. Just as medieval minds envisaged a great chain of being, which stretched from earthly imperfection to celestial resplendence, so I envision existence in terms of a great bookshelf, with one author leading us through life to the next. The purpose of this chapter, however, is not to lead you to one more book, but to twenty-two more books!

The following titles are all recommended reads for those who feel as though they're going through their own winter with God.

The Cost of Discipleship by Dietrich Bonhoeffer

The Cost of a Discipleship is a cranky classic. Much like *The Imitation of Christ,* it bosses you around, but deep down you know it's for your own good. This is the kind of book that remedies cheap grace with tough love, telling its readers, "Discipleship means adherence to Jesus Christ alone, and immediately." The fact that its author took up his cross— rather than the swastika—and followed Jesus into the heart of Nazi Germany (to his untimely death) adds a measure of gravity to everything Bonhoeffer has written.

Catechism of the Catholic Church

Wisdom is found in many wonderful places. Regardless of your theological tradition, the *Catechism of the Catholic Church* can provide countless insights and thoughtful reflections on matters of faith and morals. Read through it and discover the inspiration of the Holy Spirit, as filtered through the words of Scripture, the weight of tradition, the sanctity of the saints, the genius of great minds, and the guidance of the Magisterium. Read it and be enriched.

Pilgrim at Tinker Creek by Annie Dillard

Annie Dillard's Pulitzer Prize-winning masterpiece is on par with (or better than) anything written by Henry David Thoreau or Ralph Waldo Emerson. Dillard's work is a first-class read for anyone who takes pleasure in nature (she singlehandedly put nature writing back on the American literary map). In it, she intricately blends the natural with the theological and philosophical, creating an exceptionally honest and examining work about God's place in and outside of nature.

Devotions upon Emergent Occasions and *Death's Duel* by John Donne

John Donne wrote movingly about his mortality on two very different occasions. The first was a series of meditations he composed in the wake of a life-threatening bout of typhus. These contain some of the English language's most poignant and memorable lines, such as "No man is an island" and "For whom the bell tolls." Donne survived this sickness and lived for another seven years. The second piece happened to be his last, which was a sermon entitled "Death's Duel." Compared to *Devotions upon Emergent Occasions,* this sermon is more serene and hopeful. Although this sermon isn't as well known as Donne's other work, it comes just as highly recommended. There are few writers who address the same subject with as much experience, exquisiteness, and insight.

Bad Religion by Ross Douthat

Ross Douthat is a leading columnist for the *New York Times* and one of North America's most reliable and perceptive analysts of contemporary religion. *Bad Religion* offers a helpful diagnosis of what went wrong in the American religious scene and finishes with a hopeful prescription for how to revive good, robust forms of Christianity. If you want to know more about what people believe today—mistaking it as religion—this is the book to read.

Silence by Shūsaku End

This novel is essential reading for anyone who knows a Judas or has felt like one. Written by one of Japan's finest authors, *Silence* is about two seventeenth-century Jesuits who embark on a missionary endeavor to evangelize Japan at a time when Christianity is being systematically persecuted. The novel speaks to the silence of God amidst the toll of persecution and loss, but also to God's hidden mercies amidst our most desperate moments.

Celebration of Discipline by Richard J. Foster

The title of Foster's book does little to recommend itself, but it is nevertheless a worthwhile read. This classic text offers brief but stimulating introductions to the various spiritual practices, or disciplines, of the Christian tradition. These range from meditation and fasting to solitude and confession. Some disciplines will be more appealing than others. And some will be entirely unappetizing like fasting. But a million copies on the *Celebration of Discipline* still remains a must-read for low and high churchgoers alike.

The Power and the Glory by Graham Greene

Greene tells the story of a compromised "whiskey priest" on the run in revolutionary Mexico (who happens to be hiding from more than the police). The novel offers valuable insights into the perils of religious respectability and demonstrates how faithfulness despite our failures is its own form of sanctity.

The Imitation of Christ by Thomas à Kempis

In devotional literature, there is no school of the spirit that is superior to *The Imitation of Christ*. This has been one of the most popular and revered books in the Christian tradition (other than the Bible) for the past five hundred years. But be warned: it isn't a book for the faint of heart. It was written in the 1400s for the benefit of monks—the type that didn't get out much or look too kindly on the things of this world—so don't be surprised if you get some unsalutary advice. But this book is a field of pearls. Where else but in *The Imitation of Christ* will you be bluntly told, "All human glory, all temporal honor, all worldly acclaim, when compared to Your eternal glory, is but stupid foolishness"?

Spiritual Writings by Søren Kierkegaard

Kierkegaard is one of the modern era's greatest minds, and in this book of spiritual writings, he explores the words of Scripture with childlike credulity. These are the reflections of a man who really believes everything Jesus said and who understands a great deal more than most of us can comprehend. It also makes for a fascinating study having the philosophical founder of existentialism and the author of *The Concept of Anxiety* write with complete seriousness about how to emulate the ease and serenity of the birds of the air and the lilies of the field, who lack all anxiety and "neither toil nor spin" (Matthew 6:28).

Mere Christianity by C. S. Lewis

One of the chief reasons we feel God's absence is our ignorance of Him. God is so often shrouded in a cloud of unknowing. So we should take every opportunity we're presented with to study what is already known about Him. Yet even this can be difficult since there are differences of opinion, but C. S. Lewis' *Mere Christianity* masterfully presents a form of Christianity that we can all agree on. Some parts of the book may sound dated. But the author's erudition remains second to none, and his ideas continue to inspire or provoke today's saints and skeptics.

The Problem of Pain and *A Grief Observed* by C. S. Lewis

C. S. Lewis wrote two books about pain. *The Problem of Pain* was his first, written in 1940, and it offers the Oxford don's precise and penetrating theories on the subject. It is a tour de force in defense of God. The second, *A Grief Observed*, was written twenty years later from a polar opposite point of view. Lewis wrote it in the wake of his wife's premature passing, and it is a deeply personal and painful book, which Lewis hurled at God. Taken together, these two books offer a rounded view of the experience of pain. They also encapsulate what T. S. Eliot wrote in *Little Gidding*: "We shall not cease from exploration, and the end of all our exploring will be to arrive where we started and know the place for the first time."[2]

No Man Is an Island by Thomas Merton

No Man Is an Island is the finest distillation of monastic wisdom available for those outside the monastery since *The Imitation of Christ.* It is also more accessible to modern readers than *The Imitation,* because Merton wrote in the twentieth century rather the fifteenth. This book contains profound meditations on the hidden dynamics of devotion but wisely notes, "The saint must see the truth as something to serve, not as something to own and manipulate according to his own good pleasure."

Revelations of Divine Love (short text) by Julian of Norwich

If, at the end of all your reading and all your searching, you still do not know the answers to life's deepest questions—or even the middling ones—the spiritual experiences and ecstasies of Julian of Norwich are worth reading. She's not necessarily your "every woman," but the pure devotion of this beautiful medieval mystic has been an inspiration to many people, including T. S. Eliot. Her account of Christ's visitations is deeply inspiring—if at times slightly alarming. But in the end, the reader is calmed and convinced by Christ's promise to Julian that "all shall be well, and all shall be well and all manner of things shall be well."

Let Your Life Speak: Listening for the Voice of Vocation by Parker J. Palmer

Living a life of purpose is part of the purpose of life. Finding out what that purpose is—which is one's vocation—is the key to unlocking, not all, but a lot of life's happiness. One of the merits of Palmer's work is that it's in touch with the Holy

Spirit, so he's not suggesting that it's all about us. This is a beautiful book that has the potential to add integrity, purpose, and spiritual meaning to your deepest desires and your life's longest labors.

Pensées by Blaise Pascal

Pensées (French for "thoughts") is a unique work that is highly regarded, but rarely read. Which is what Mark Twain referred to as a "classic" book. Pascal was a precocious genius who studied lots but was often sick and died quite young. During his short life, he made major contributions in math and science, as well as in literature and religion. His *Pensées* belong to his latter accomplishments (although it was posthumously published). It is a series of loosely connected aphoristic thoughts on things like human nature, personal knowledge, divine mysteries, and the Christian religion, besides much else. *Pensées* is a landmark in French literature and one of the most original and thought provoking works of reflection ever written.

Jesus through the Centuries by Jaroslav Pelikan

This is one of the most readable intellectual histories about the Christian/Western tradition. Follow Christ through the centuries of Western civilization and see how His teaching and example have inspired divergent and devout minds alike, ranging from Augustine and Aquinas to Tolstoy and Martin Luther King Jr., revealing all the while that the life of the mind is seldom far from the life of Christ.

On the Shortness of Life by Seneca

Seneca wrote that life is long if you know how to use it. He should know, because he was one of Rome's greatest philosophers and politicians. This essay is perhaps the earliest time management advice ever written and possibly still the best. It contains invaluable lessons on what time should mean to us, why we waste so much of it, and how we can properly prioritize the important things in life. Time is God's gift to us, and if we use it wisely, we'll be rewarded with infinitely more of it.

Prayer: Does It Make Any Difference? by Philip Yancey

Philip Yancey has a terrific capacity for perceiving and exploring the micro and macro landscapes of prayer. This book covers everything from Yancey's responses to personal letters about terrible pain and unanswered prayer, to the powerful impact of public prayer on global events like the fall of the Berlin Wall. He has a journalist's eye for details, a philosopher's mind for ideas, a pastor's heart for people, and a writer's hand for readability—what more could you ask for on such an important subject as prayer?

What's So Amazing about Grace? by Philip Yancey

By the end of this book, you'll find yourself wondering what *isn't* amazing about grace. There is so much to appreciate and admire about this generous and uplifting book. It powerfully impresses upon the reader 101 ways in which God's grace is operating in the world to make it livable, lovable, and luminous. *What's So Amazing about Grace?* is also an open challenge to the church to be as gracious to others as God is to the world.

Sole Survivor by Philip Yancey

For an avid reader, the best book is a book about books. In *Sole Survivor,* Yancey explores his life's bookshelf through the dual roles of autobiographer and book critic. He tells his own stories—about things like his bigoted upbringing and his life as a writer—while delving into the lives and thoughts of the authors that impacted him. The book is enjoyable as a whole, but it's also well suited to being picked apart author by author. Among the most stimulating profiles are Yancey's treatment of Annie Dillard, Frederick Buechner (who is a must-read), John Donne, and Shūsaku Endō.

Acknowledgments

A lot more goes into a book than writing. It is the product of many people's contributions, and this book belongs to them all.

Let me begin by acknowledging that insofar as this book is true and helpful, it was written as much by God as by me. Through an abundance of grace and inspiration, I gladly became the junior partner in this project.

Winter with God would not have been possible without my family. Peter, Joanne, Fergus, and Christianne: for a lifetime of love, friendship, and encouragement, both the book and its author are forever in your kind and gracious debt.

I would also like to thank Eugene Peterson. His early work on the Psalms (as chronicled in *The Pastor*) inspired me to write this book. Then later, at a moment in the writing process when I was all but defeated, an apparently chance encounter with Peterson restored my perseverance. Thank you for telling me to just keep writing.

Winter with God began as a weekly devotional for my then local church. Had David Zimmerman—pastor and friend—not embraced this idea, the book itself might never have materialized. Likewise, without Michelle Thompson, these devotionals would not have actually made it into the weekly bulletin.

The first draft of this book owes a lot to Aubrey Driedger. He often endured my writer's wroth, as he was not afraid to critique my work, and I surely profited by his perseverance. Similarly, David Parker served as an ever-present, ever-faithful sounding board from inception to completion. He is a writer's true wingman. Lastly, I have Richard Kemick to thank for self-lessly spending time editing my manuscript to make it more serviceable.

While studying at Regent College—and writing this book on my weekends—I received help and encouragement from numerous sources. David Brooks, Frank Klassen, Rajan Matthew, Duncan Ris, Matthew Thomas, Kevin Greenlee, Becky Pruitt, Don Lewis, J. I. Packer, Bill Reimer, and Bruce and Carolyn Hindmarsh all blessed me in their own way, whether they realized it or not.

While in Vancouver, the Williamses—Sarah, Paul, Emilia, and Hannah—opened their house to me (including their cabin on Galiano Island) and became my family away from home. Sarah has provided a great deal of technical and personal assistance, which has proven invaluable for both the book and its author.

I would also like to acknowledge those who provided early endorsements, such as Mike Mason, J. I. Packer, Sarah Williams, Gary Thomas, and Jennifer Rees Larcombe. Likewise, I also owe a big thank-you to those who provided me with introductions and served as intermediaries.

I am greatly indebted to the prayerful support of my local church and *Winter with God* prayer team. Likewise, I am grateful for the love and support of my godmother, Penny Thomas, and such friends as Spencer and Ellie, Jordan and Britney, Seth and Carly, Toph, Hunter, Josh, Andrew, Edu, and many more.

Sometimes I'm not sure which is harder: writing a book or getting it published. There is little doubt, however, that without the help of John Stackhouse, Lynn Szabo, and (again) Mike Mason, this book would not have been published at all. For without them I wouldn't have had contacts to approach or a proposal to offer. Similarly, I would be nowhere without the representation of Dan Balow and the Steve Laube Agency. I am grateful that you took a chance on me when others passed. So too, I appreciate the entire team at BroadStreet for making *Winter with God* a reality. I've enjoyed working with everyone, such as David Sluka and Bill Watkins. Indeed, it has been a privilege to partner with all of you.

Notes

Spiritual Winter

1. Ernest Hemingway, *A Movable Feast* (London: Arrow Books, 2009), 39.
2. William Shakespeare, *Richard III* (Oxford: Oxford University Press, 2008) I, i, 1.
3. Frank Loesser, "Baby, It's Cold Outside," 1944.
4. Ralph Waldo Emerson, "Beauty," in *Nature* (New York: Penguin, 2008), 11.

Devotion 2

1. Friedrich Nietzsche, *Twilight of the Idols and the Anti-Christ* (New York: Penguin, 1990), 3.
2. Adam Gopnik, *Winter* (Toronto: Anansi, 2011), 178.
3. Ibid.

Devotion 4

1. C. S. Lewis, *The Four Loves* (New York: Harcourt Trade, 1971), 6.
2. Jean Vanier, *Signs: Seven Wonders of Hope* (Toronto: Novalis, 2013).

Devotion 5

1. Thomas Merton, *No Man Is an Island* (New York: Harcourt, 1983), 45.
2. William Shakespeare, *Romeo and Juliet* (Oxford: Oxford University Press, 2008), II, ii, 1.
3. "Mark Twain," BrainyQuote.com, Xplore Inc., http://www.brainyquote.com/quotes/quotes/m/marktwain137915.html.

Devotion 9

1. Blaise Pascal, *Pensées* (New York: Penguin, 1995), 37.
2. Saint Augustine, *Confessions* (Oxford: Oxford University Press, 1998), 187.
3. Ralph Waldo Emerson, "Nature," in *Nature and Selected Essays* (New York: Classic Books International, 2010), 5.

Devotion 10

1. Dietrich Bonhoeffer, *Life Together* (New York: HarperCollins, 1954), 111.
2. Ibid., 116.

Devotion 12

1. Hans Urs von Balthasar, *Prayer* (San Francisco: Ignatius Press, 1986), 14.
2. John Cassian, *Conferences,* trans. Colm Luibheid (New York: Paulist Press, 1985), 9.14.

Devotion 16

1. Augustine, *Confessions*, 145.

Devotion 20

1. Thomas à Kempis, *The Imitation of Christ* (New York: Vintage, 1998), 5.
2. Charles Spurgeon, "Paul—His Cloak and His Books," The Spurgeon Archive, http://www.spurgeon.org/sermons/0542.php.

Devotion 21

1. Pierre Teilhard de Chardin, "Patient Trust," *Ignatian Spirituality* (blog), posted on November 23, 2010, http://www.ignatianspirituality.com/8078/prayer-of-theilhard-de-chardin.

Devotion 22 or 23

1. Bonhoeffer, *Life Together,* 54.

Devotion 24

1. Fyodor Dostoevsky, *Memoirs from the House of the Dead* (Oxford: Oxford University Press, 2008), pt. 1, ch. 1.
2. Helen H. Lemmel, "Turn Your Eyes upon Jesus," 1922.
3. C. S. Lewis, *Mere Christianity* (New York: HarperCollins, 2001), 134.
4. T. S. Eliot, "Little Gidding," from *Four Quartets* (New York: Harcourt, Brace and Co., 1943), III.

Devotion 25

1. Pierre Teilhard de Chardin, in *The Joy of Kindness*, Robert J. Furey (New York: Crossroad Publishing Co., 1993), 138.

Devotion 26

1. Pascal, "Diversion," *Pensées*, 136.

Devotion 27

1. Samuel Johnson, "Consolation in the Face of Death," in *Consolation in the Face of Death* (New York: Penguin, 2009), 114.
2 Ronald Head, "C. S. Lewis as a Parishioner," in Roger White, Judith Wolfe, and Brendan N. Wolfe, eds., *C. S. Lewis and His Circle* (Oxford University Press, 2015), 185.
3 Kempis, *The Imitation of Christ*, 34.

Devotion 28

1. William Shakespeare, "Sonnet 29," in *The Complete Sonnets and Poems* (Oxford: Oxford University Press, 2008), 439.

Devotion 31

1. C. S. Lewis, *God in the Dock* (Grand Rapids: Wm. B. Eerdmans, 2014), 210.
2. Augustine, *Confessions*, 3.

Devotion 34

1. Lord Byron, *Manfred* (Cambridge: Harvard University Press, 1914), 1, i, 13.
2. Merton, *No Man Is an Island,* 198.

Devotion 35

1. Søren Kierkegaard, quoted in Malcolm Muggeridge, *A Third Testament* (New York: The Plough Publishing House, 2011), 65.

Devotion 36

1. Joseph M. Scriven, "What a Friend We Have in Jesus," 1855.

Devotion 38

1. William Shakespeare, *Henry IV, Part II*, ed. René Weis (Oxford: Oxford University Press, 2009), III, I, 31.

Devotion 40

1. C. S. Lewis, "Learning in Wartime," in *The Weight of Glory* (San Francisco: HarperCollins, 2001), 49.

Conclusion

1. Thomas More, in *The Oxford Book of Prayer*, ed. George Appleton (Oxford: Oxford University Press, 2009), 123.
2. T. S. Eliot, "The Hollow Men," v. 5–9.

Winter with God: A Reading List

1 Saint Augustine, *Confessions*, 152.
2 T. S. Eliot, "Little Gidding," vv. 26–29

About the Author

photo by: Duncan Ris

T. W. S. Hunt was born in England and immigrated to Canada in 1999. He lives in the foothills of the Rocky Mountains. An avid learner, he studied history at Trinity Western University and the University of Oxford. He later acquired a bachelor of education at the University of British Columbia, and an MA in theological studies from Regent College. He has worked in the Canadian Prime Minister's Office and at *The American Interest* magazine. T. W. S. Hunt is ecumenical in his faith and has been blessed by many different denominations. In his free time, he enjoys hiking, snowshoeing, reading, music, movies, and spending time with family and friends.

To inquire about booking T. W. S. Hunt for speaking engagements or retreat leadership, please email twshunt.contact @gmail.com. For more information and to stay connected, visit facebook.com/twshuntauthor.